RY
O. THE BIBLE

William MacDonald

LUKE 24:27

**Original text material by William McDonald.
Developed as a correspondence course by Emmaus
Correspondence School, founded in 1942.**

111213/040302

ISBN 0-940293-59-5

© 1954, 1970 William MacDonald

Printed in the United States of America

Instructions to Students

This course has been written primarily for two classes of people.

First of all, it is for those who know little or nothing about the Bible, but who would like to become familiar with this Book of all books. There are many such people who honestly approach the Scriptures with a real desire to study them, but who get discouraged because of the size of the Book and because of their ignorance of what it is all about. They feel that if they just had a general summary of the story of the Bible, they would be better able to read it and understand it. In these lessons, therefore, an attempt has been made to give a brief outline of the contents of God's Word.

Secondly, it is for those who are familiar with individual Bible incidents, but who do not know how to piece them together or fit them into the historical background. For instance, many folks have heard the story of Daniel in the lions' den from early childhood, yet they would be at a loss to explain the time and location of this incident in the record of God's dealing with His people, Israel. For these people, the well-known stories of the Bible are shown in their proper setting, with an explanation of their importance at that particular time.

It will be very obvious to every student that these lessons deal only with what might be called the mountain-peaks of Scripture. In fact, we hope that the amount of material omitted and the number of questions unanswered will prove to be so painful that the student will have an increased determination to study the Word more thoroughly when he completes this course! It is also our hope that this course may prove suggestive to Sunday School and Bible Class teachers in their work of teaching others.

In order to derive the greatest benefit from the course, the student should read the portion of Scripture covered by each lesson.

LESSONS YOU WILL STUDY

1. The Story Begins (Genesis—Exodus)
2. On To Canaan (Leviticus—Joshua)
3. We Want a King! (Judges—2 Samuel)
4. The Downfall of the Monarchy (Kings—Esther)
5. "Give Me Thy Heart" (Job—Song of Solomon)
6. The Major Prophets (Isaiah—Daniel)
7. The Minor Prophets (Hosea—Micah)
8. More Minor Prophets (Nahum—Malachi)
9. Christ and His Church (The Gospels and The Acts)
10. From the Pen of Paul (Romans—Galatians)
11. More Letters From Paul (Ephesians—Philemon)
12. Look Out! Look Up! (Hebrews—Revelation)

HOW TO STUDY

Begin by asking God to open your heart to receive the truths He would teach you from His Word. Read the lesson through at least twice, once to get the general drift of its contents and then again, slowly, looking up all Scripture references and examining all footnotes.

EXAMS AND SELF-CHECK TESTS

All lessons are followed by Self-Check Tests. Every second lesson is also followed by an exam. Before taking the Self-Check Tests and Exams you may use them for reviewing the lesson. However, when you actually come to take the exams you should do so without reference to the lesson, your Bible or your notebook unless otherwise instructed. *Read the following instructions carefully.*

1. Self-Check Tests

These are in the form of ten True or False questions dealing with the factual content of the lesson you have just studied. They will help you evaluate your progress before you take the exam and go on to the next lesson. A complete Answer Key to these Self-Check Tests will be found at the back of this book. When you have answered all the questions, check and score your answers. Re-study areas where you made mistakes. *DO NOT SEND SELF-CHECK TESTS TO THE CORRESPONDENCE SCHOOL.* Grade them yourself.

2. Exams

Each exam covers two lessons. (Exam 1, for example, covers lessons 1 and 2.) Each exam is clearly marked to show you which questions deal with which lesson. You may take the exam in two stages. When you have completed lesson 1, you may take the part of Exam 1 dealing with that lesson. Do not mail the exam to the School, however, until you have completed lesson 2 and taken the second part of the exam. *NEVER SEND IN AN EXAM FOR CORRECTION UNTIL BOTH PARTS ARE COMPLETED.* Send in an exam for correction as soon as you have completed all of it.

You may use any version of the Bible for general study. When answering exam questions, however, restrict yourself to either the *Authorized (King James) Version* (1611), or the *American Standard Version* (1901). These are two widely used versions. There are so many versions today that your instructor cannot possibly check them all in evaluating your work.

3. Thought and Research Questions

Some exams contain questions designed to make you do original Bible study. You may use your Bible to answer these questions. They are clearly marked.

4. What Do You Say? Questions

Questions headed in this way are optional and no point value is assigned to them. You may freely state your own opinions in answer to such questions. Your candid answers will help your instructor get to know you better as an individual. They will also help us evaluate the general effectiveness of this course.

5. How Your Papers Are Graded

Any incorrectly answered questions will be marked by your instructor. You will be referred back to the place in the Bible or the textbook where the correct answer is to be found.

RECORD YOUR GRADES

When you send in your first exam a Grade Record Card will be returned to you showing your grade for the lesson(s) just corrected. You must return this card to the School each time you send in further exams.

GROUP ENROLLMENTS

If you are enrolled in a class, submit your exam papers to the leader or secretary of the class who will send them for the entire group to the Correspondence School.

Class leaders should see the special suggestions for using the Self-Check Tests in a group situation. These suggestions are given on the front page of the Answer Key to the Self-Check Tests at the end of this book.

GENERAL INSTRUCTIONS

Begin studying immediately or, if you are in a group, as soon as the group begins. Try to keep a regular study schedule. You will be allowed a maximum of one year to complete this course from the time of enrollment.

The Story Begins

GENESIS

The Bible is not a history of the world nor of the human race. Its contents have been divinely selected to show the development of God's purposes for man and for his salvation. Therefore, some major historical events are omitted and some minor incidents are included because of their bearing on these divine purposes.

The principal subjects dealt with in the first book of the Bible are the Creation, the Fall, the Flood, the Tower of Babel, Abraham, Isaac, Jacob and Joseph.

The only reliable statement of the origin of man and of the universe in which he lives is given in the first two chapters of Genesis. Then follows the record of the entrance of sin into the human race through Adam and Eve in the Garden of Eden. At this time, God gave a promise of the coming of Christ (3:15). During the rest of the Old Testament narrative, we are able to trace the human descent of the Savior of the world; it is one of the most important threads in the Bible.

For centuries after the Fall, man's career was steadily downward, until God sent the Flood upon the earth and destroyed all its inhabitants except Noah and his family. This event took place at least 1600 years after Adam's creation, possibly more. After the Flood men again rebelled against God and expressed their defiance in the building of the Tower of Babel. God's judgment, this time, was to confound human speech and scatter the human race to the ends of the earth.

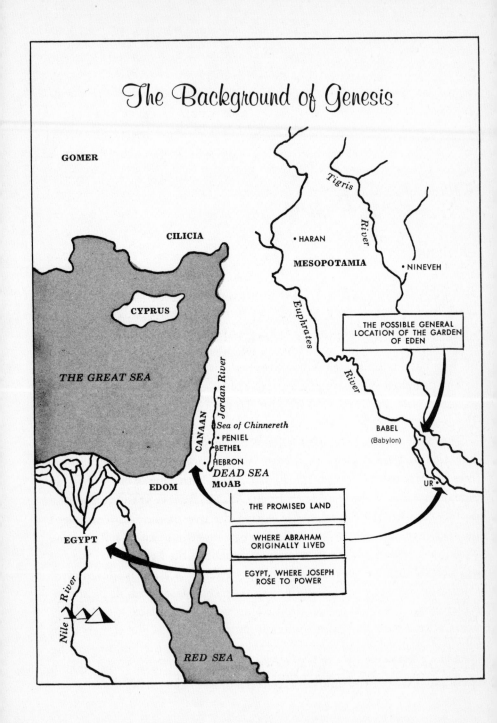

In chapter 12—400 years after Noah—God called Abraham from Ur of the Chaldees.[1] This is important because it marks the beginning of God's chosen earthly people, Israel. God promised Abraham that he would be the father of a great nation, that the Messiah would be descended from him, and that his people would be given the land of Canaan as their possession. Actually almost all the remaining narrative of the Old Testament is devoted to God's dealings with this people. Also, beginning with chapter 13, the scene of most of the events is the land of Canaan except for two main exiles which will be noted.

We are next told of Abraham's son, Isaac—his birth, his escape from death on Mt. Moriah, and his marriage to Rebekah. Their two sons were Esau and Jacob, and it is the latter who now assumes the leading role.

Many incidents in the life of Jacob are recorded, all of them full of valuable lessons for the reader. However, the important fact about him, as far as the progress of the history is concerned, is that he was the father of twelve sons who, in turn, became heads of what are henceforth known as the twelve tribes of Israel.[2] In the order of their birth, these sons were Reuben, Simeon, Levi, Judah, Dan, Naphtali, Gad, Asher, Issachar, Zebulun, Joseph, Benjamin.

It is with Joseph that the narrative is next concerned. He was not an ancestor of the Lord Jesus Christ,[3] but in his life and work, he presents more types and pictures of the Savior than almost any other Old Testament character. Though loved by his father, Joseph was hated by his brothers and sold by them to a caravan of merchants en route to Egypt. In that country, he quickly rose to prominence in the government of Pharaoh. When a famine hit Canaan years later, the sons of Jacob heard that there was food in Egypt, so they went there for help and eventually moved there as a family. The Book of Genesis closes with the death of Joseph in Egypt, about 270 years after the call of Abraham.

---

[1] Chaldea is later mentioned in the Bible as Babylonia. This is known today as Iraq.
[2] The entire nation is often referred to hereafter as Israel.
[3] The Messiah was descended from his brother, Judah.

EXODUS

After Joseph's death, a new Pharaoh came to power in Egypt who was unfriendly to the Hebrew people, and who reduced them to slavery. Moses was raised up by God during these years to stand before Pharaoh and demand freedom for the Israelites to return to Canaan. When the ruler refused, God sent a series of nine plagues upon Egypt, all of which failed to convince him; he was unwilling to let the people go.

Finally, God announced the tenth plague—the death of the oldest boy in every home in Egypt that was not protected by the blood of the Passover lamb. The Egyptians failed to comply with God's demands so death struck every family. The Israelites, having the blood on the doors, were spared. Under the leadership of Moses, they left Egypt in haste, with Pharaoh's army after them. The Lord miraculously parted the waters of the Red Sea so that His people could get across, and so that the pursuing army would be drowned in trying to follow.

Abraham's family, through Isaac, his son, and Jacob, his grandson, had now become a nation of about two million people, unified and organized for their journey to the Promised Land. Think of this tremendous host marching through a great wilderness, with flocks and herds, camping at various spots en route! God guided His people with a pillar of cloud by day and a pillar of fire by night. Then He miraculously provided food for them by raining manna[1] from heaven. Three months after leaving Egypt, they arrived at the Desert of Sinai, where they were destined to remain for a while.

The Israelites encamped near Mt. Sinai,[2] and stayed there for nearly a year. In fact, all the events recorded from Exodus 19 to Numbers 10: 11 occurred at this location.

Now that Abraham's family had become a nation, it needed a system of laws to regulate its behavior when it came into its own land. But more than that, God had important lessons to teach His people about His holiness, about their sinfulness and how He could be approached.

---

[1] A small, round white substance which the Israelites found on the ground each morning, and which they used to make bread or cakes.
[2] Also called Mt. Horeb. It is located in today's Sinai Pennisula.

First of all, then, God issued the Ten Commandments to Moses for Israel. These form the basis of much human government. In addition to these, He gave various other laws concerning man's obligations toward the Lord and toward his fellow men.

Then God issued very detailed instructions concerning the building of the tabernacle, a tent-like structure where He would meet with His people, and which would therefore form the center of the religious life of the nation. The materials used in constructing the tabernacle, the furniture inside—in fact, almost all things connected with it—were typical of the person and work of the Lord Jesus who was to come.

Closely connected with the tabernacle was the priesthood. Therefore, God next arranged for an order of priests to be taken from the tribe of Levi, and the family of Aaron, Moses' brother. Their clothing, their work and the ceremonies connected with their entrance into the priestly office are minutely described.

While Moses was still in Mt. Sinai receiving the law from God, the people of Israel broke the law by making a golden calf and worshipping it. When Moses returned and saw this, he broke the stone tablets on which the law was written, then pleaded with God not to destroy the people. After this, God again gave the law to Moses on the mount, this time accompanying it with promises of grace and mercy.

The people now came forward with their free-will offerings and undertook the work of building the tabernacle. When it was completed, the priests were set apart and clothed, and all was now in readiness. A bright, shining cloud covered the tent, indicating God's presence with His people.

The Book of Exodus is filled with instructive pictures of our own lives.

1. The Passover speaks of salvation through the blood of Christ.
2. Crossing the Red Sea pictures the Christian saying good-bye to the world, and living in practical separation from it.
3. The tabernacle and its services tell of how the believer approaches God in worship.
4. The Priesthood illustrates how our Great High Priest, the Lord Jesus, represents us before the Throne of God.

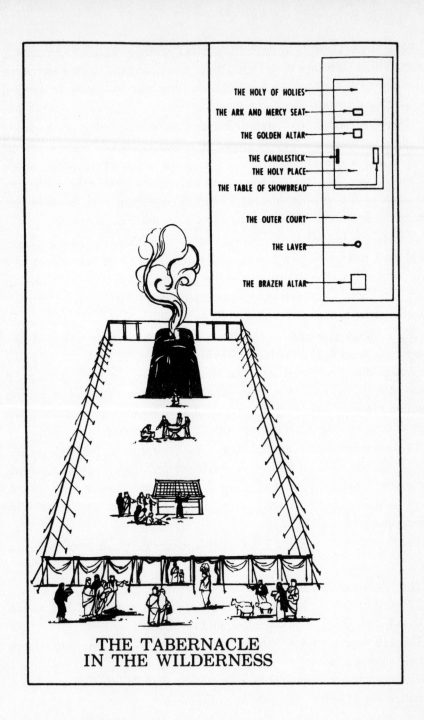

THE HOLY OF HOLIES

THE ARK AND MERCY SEAT

THE GOLDEN ALTAR

THE CANDLESTICK

THE HOLY PLACE

THE TABLE OF SHOWBREAD

THE OUTER COURT

THE LAVER

THE BRAZEN ALTAR

THE TABERNACLE
IN THE WILDERNESS

When you have mastered this lesson, take the Self-Check Test on page 1/8. Look up the answers to this test and see how well you did.

Then take the first part of Exam 1 (covering lesson 1), questions 1-10 on pages 2/9-11 (right after lesson 2).

SELF CHECK TEST 1

RECALL WHAT YOU HAVE LEARNED

In the right-hand margin circle the following statements "True" or "False":

1. The history of the Children of Israel begins with the call of Abraham (p. 1./3). (T)   F

2. The father of the twelve boys who founded the Twelve Tribes of Israel was Jacob (p. 1/3). (T)   F

3. The great river of Mesopotamia on which was located Ur, Abraham's original home, was the Tigris (p. 1/2). T   (F)

4. The Son of Jacob who rose from slavery to high eminence in the court of Pharaoh in Egypt was Judah (p. 1/4). T   (F)

5. God visited the Egyptians with ten plagues altogether before Pharaoh finally liberated the Israelites from slavery (p. 1/4). (T)   F

6. In Egypt the Children of Israel multiplied in number from the size of a family to a nation of about two million people (p. 1/4). (T)   F

7. The Law of Moses comprised only the Ten Commandments (p. 1/5). T   (F)

8. When the Tabernacle was erected the only piece of furniture placed in the Holy of Holies was the ark with its mercy seat (p. 1/6). (T)   F

9. The priests of Israel were taken from the leading families of all the Tribes (p. 1/5). T   (F)

10. The Tabernacle and its services illustrate the way God is to be approached (p. 1/5). (T)   F

Turn to the end of the book for the answers to these questions. Do NOT send them to the Correspondence School.

On To Canaan

LEVITICUS

This book is a manual of instructions for the priests, given to Moses by the Lord as He spoke from the tabernacle while the people were still camping at Sinai. The main contents of the book may be summarized as follows:

1. The five offerings—burnt, meal, peace, sin and trespass—which the people through their priests were to bring to the Lord as sacrifice. These all set forth the death of Christ in different ways.
2. The ceremonies which the priests had to observe in order to fit them for their important duties.
3. Laws concerning animals which could be used by the Jews as food, and other animals, like pigs, which were unclean.
4. Laws concerning personal cleanliness, and chastity, both of men and women.
5. Instructions concerning the detection and treatment of leprosy.
6. Regulations concerning the great solemn, holy days of the nation, namely (a) the Sabbath, (b) the Passover Feast, (c) the Feast of Unleavened Bread, (d) the Feast of Firstfruits, (e) the Feast of Weeks, or Pentecost, (f) the Feast of Trumpets, (g) the Day of Atonement, and (h) the Feast of Tabernacles.

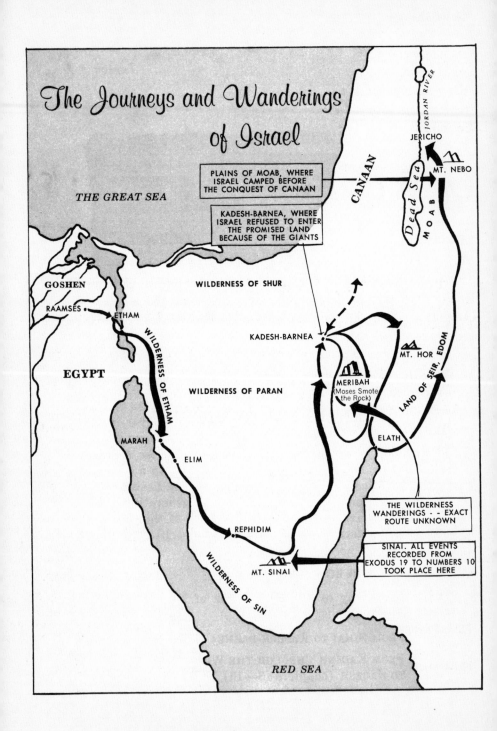

NUMBERS

As already mentioned, the events described in Numbers 1 through 10:
11 took place at Sinai. These chapters describe various preparations of
the nation to pack up and march on to Canaan. The most important
requirement was to number the people so that they could be arranged
in an orderly way for the procession.

After camping for about a year at Sinai, the nation began its journey.
Its behavior was characterized by complaints, rebellions and unbelief.
Finally, the sin of the people reached a climax at Kadesh-Barnea when
they sent spies into Canaan to see what it was like. God had already
promised the land to them, and assured them that He would drive out
their enemies. Yet all but two of the spies, Caleb and Joshua, reported
that the enemies were unconquerable.

As a result of this evil report and the subsequent murmuring of the
people, God decreed that:

1. the people would wander in the wilderness for 40 years before they
   would reach Canaan.
2. of all the people 20 years old and above, only Caleb and Joshua
   would ever enter the land. The rest would perish in the wilderness.

The history of this prolonged wandering is almost unrecorded in the
Scriptures. Two incidents of importance are mentioned, however.

1. Because of an act of disobedience at Meribah, Moses was prevented
   from going into Canaan with his people.
2. Because of their murmuring, the Israelites were plagued with fiery
   serpents. They were saved by looking at a brass serpent which Moses
   lifted up on a pole.

After their many years of futile travel, the people returned to
Kadesh-Barnea, then started to journey to the plains of Moab where
they camped before entering the Promised Land. There a final census
was taken, and directions were given as to the division of the land.

DEUTERONOMY

Now that the people are about to go into Canaan, God must instruct

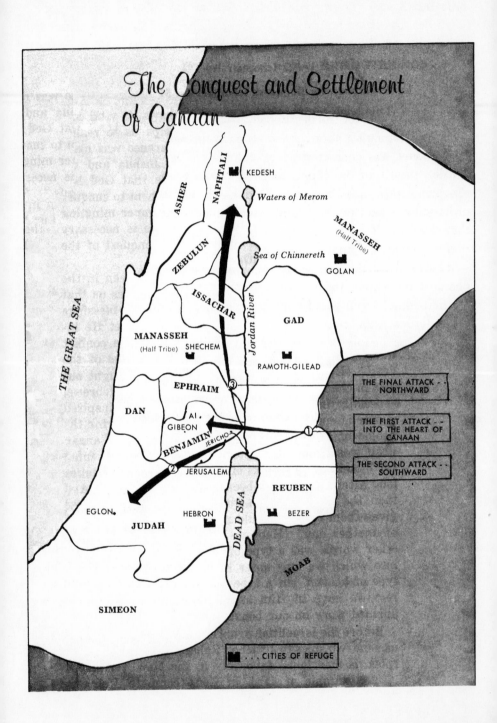

The Conquest and Settlement of Canaan

THE GREAT SEA

ASHER
NAPHTALI
KEDESH
Waters of Merom
MANASSEH (Half Tribe)
ZEBULUN
Sea of Chinnereth
GOLAN
ISSACHAR
Jordan River
GAD
MANASSEH (Half Tribe)
SHECHEM
RAMOTH-GILEAD
EPHRAIM
③   THE FINAL ATTACK - - NORTHWARD
DAN
AI
GIBEON
①   THE FIRST ATTACK - - INTO THE HEART OF CANAAN
BENJAMIN
JERICHO
②   THE SECOND ATTACK - - SOUTHWARD
JERUSALEM
REUBEN
EGLON
HEBRON
BEZER
DEAD SEA
JUDAH
MOAB
SIMEON

■ . . . CITIES OF REFUGE

them thoroughly. They could only enjoy the land if they understood God's dealings, were acquainted with His thoughts, and were obedient to His will.

Thus we find Moses rehearsing their past history and reviewing the law. He faithfully urges them to be obedient and warns them against idolatry and intermingling with the heathen nations. Inasmuch as a new generation had arisen since the march to Canaan began, it was imperative that they learn from past mistakes, and also that they be familiar with the law.

In addition to this, Moses gave them additional laws and instructions concerning their behavior in the land, with especial reference to idolatry, worship, false prophets, selection of a king and wars. The results of obedience and disobedience were given in detail.

In the closing chapters of the book, the future of Israel is foretold; then Moses blesses the twelve tribes as the time of his death draws near. The Lord buries his body in an unknown grave in Moab, and Joshua is appointed leader in his place.

JOSHUA

Joshua was faced with the task of invading Canaan, destroying its heathen inhabitants, dividing the land among the tribes of Israel and otherwise settling the people in their homeland.

By way of preparation, he reminded the people that although the land was theirs, they must go in and possess it. The heathen occupants, known as Canaanites, Hittites, Amorites, Perizzites, Hivites, Jebusites, etc., must be utterly killed, both to punish them for their unspeakable sins and to prevent the Jews from intermarrying with them.

Before beginning the invasion, Joshua sent spies into Jericho, the first city in the plan of attack. A woman named Rahab, though a sinner, recognized that the Israelites' God was the true God, and so befriended the spies. For this deed, she and her family were later spared from destruction.

In order to march from the Plains of Moab into Canaan, the people had to cross the Jordan River. God miraculously held back the waterflow so that the host went across on dry land. Joshua's general plan now was to drive straight into the center of the land, then attack toward the south, finally moving against the northern portion.

The mighty city of Jericho fell first. At Ai, a smaller city, the Israelites were defeated because there was sin in the camp. When this was brought to light and punished, victory followed. Directing his attention toward the south, Joshua met an allied army of five kings at Gibeon. As they fled, God smote them with hailstones, then lengthened the day so that the Jews could kill any that remained alive.

The conquest of the north centered around the waters of Merom, where the Lord gave the enemy into Joshua's hand. This campaign completed the overall plan of attack, although the Israelites failed to destroy all the inhabitants of the land.

The manner in which the land was divided is shown on the map. The tribes of Reuben and Gad and one-half of the tribe of Manasseh were given permission to settle on the east side of the Jordan. Nine and one-half tribes took up their inheritance in the land.[1]

Also shown on the map are the Cities of Refuge, three on each side of the Jordan, where one who had killed another accidentally could flee for safety. Forty-two other cities were set apart for the Levites, who ministered in the Tabernacle.

Joshua's closing address to the people before his death betrayed his uneasy feeling that they might lapse into idolatry through contact with the surviving heathen in the land.

---

[1] The tribe of Joseph's inheritance is shown under the name of Joseph's sons, Ephraim and Manasseh. The tribe of Levi did not receive a part of the land. Since they were the priestly tribe, the Lord was to be the portion of their inheritance.

When you are ready, take Self-Check Test 2 and then grade your answers.

Next complete Exam 1 by answering questions 11-20 on pages 2/12-14. (You should have already answered questions 1-10 as part of your study of lesson 1.)

SELF CHECK TEST 2

CHECK UP ON YOURSELF

In the right-hand margin circle the following statements "True" or "False":

1. According to the Law of Moses, all animals could be eaten so long as they were killed in a "kosher" fashion (p. 2/1).　　T　(F)

2. Apart from the weekly Sabbath, there were seven great annual festivals kept under the Mosaic Law (p. 2/1).　　(T)　F

3. As the Children of Israel journeyed from Sinai, their march was characterized by songs of triumph and rejoicing (p. 2/3).　　T　(F)

4. Of the twelve spies sent by Moses into Canaan to spy out the land only two brought back a completely favorable and positive report (p. 2/3).　　(T)　F

5. Because of their rebellion at Kadesh Barnea, the Children of Israel were condemned to forty years of wandering in the wilderness (p. 2/3).　　(T)　F

6. In Deuteronomy, Moses warned the younger generation, about to go on into Canaan, of the results which would follow both obedience and disobedience (p. 2/5).　　(T)　F

7. The two spies Joshua sent into Canaan to spy out the land for him were befriended by a woman named Rahab who was afterwards saved from destruction because of this act of kindness (p. 2/5).　　(T)　F

8. In order to cross the river Jordan, Joshua marched his army to its headwaters and then struck rapidly southward into Canaan (pp. 2/5, 6).　　T　(F)

9. None of the tribes were permitted to settle on the east side of Jordan (p. 2/6).　　T　(F)

10. In his closing address to Israel, Joshua warned the people against any lapse into idolatry (p. 2/6).　　(T)　F

Turn to the end of the book for the answers to these questions. Do NOT send them to the Correspondence School.

SUMMARY OF THE BIBLE

F-7

Name _Elsie Mathews_
(print plainly)

Exam Grade_____

Address_____

City_____State_____ Zip Code_____ Class Number_____

Instructor_____

LESSON 1

In the blank space in the right-hand margin write the letter of the correct answer.

1. Major historical events are omitted from the Bible because
   a. the writers of the Bible were "ignorant and unlearned men," generally speaking, and were mostly ignorant of these events
   b. the Bible is incomplete
   c. history has very little bearing on modern life
   d. the Bible does not record any history at all
   e. these events are outside the scope and purpose of the Bible   _E_

2. Which of the following describes the Bible view of Man? Man
   a. is the end product of evolution
   b. is still evolving and will continue to do so until he reaches perfection
   c. is captain of his own soul and master of his destiny
   d. is a fallen creature, ruined by sin and in need of a Savior   _D_

3. Which of the following was NOT an ancestor of the Lord Jesus?
   a. Noah
   b. Abraham
   c. Isaac
   d. Joseph
   e. Jacob   _D_

4. The greater part of the Old Testament is concerned with
   a. God's dealings with the Jewish people
   b. prophecies concerning the Lord Jesus Christ
   c. man's quest after God
   d. Church truth

5. The son of Jacob who became an ancestor of the Lord Jesus was
   a. Reuben
   b. Judah
   c. Levi
   d. Dan
   e. Benjamin
   f. Melchizedek

6. The Children of Israel were enslaved in Egypt
   a. by the Pharaoh who befriended Joseph
   b. from the time of Joseph's death until the coming of Moses
   c. because they engaged in treasonable activities with Egypt's enemies
   d. in a concentration camp where they were to be exterminated on the day of Purim

7. The Children of Israel were protected by the blood of the Passover lamb from the
   a. terrible darkness which was the chief feature of one of the plagues
   b. plague of boils
   c. the fearful lightning storm which struck Egypt on one occasion
   d. the death of the firstborn
   e. all of these

8. After their deliverance from Egypt, God led the Israelites by means of
   a. maps which Moses had taken from the Egyptian State Department
   b. bedouin shepherds who knew where the oases were in the desert and who had been befriended by Moses in the shepherd years of his life
   c. a cloudy, fiery pillar which miraculously showed them when and where to move
   d. the Urim and Thummim, special stones in the high priest's breastplate, often used for discerning God's will
   e. Jethro, Moses' father-in-law, who, knowing the desert well, went before the host as their guide   _C_

9. At Sinai, God gave the Israelites
   a. His law to show them how to order their lives
   b. military training to prepare them for the conquest of Canaan
   c. an opportunity to return to Egypt if they so desired
   d. a portion of their inheritance in the Promised Land   _A_

10. What was the great sin the Israelites committed at Sinai? They
    a. built the Tabernacle which was not to be constructed until they reached Canaan
    b. made a golden calf and worshipped it
    c. entered into a hasty alliance with the Amalekites
    d. chose a leader to take them back to Egypt because they did not know what had become of Moses
    e. ate manna, holy food reserved for the priests   _B_

WHAT DO YOU SAY?

What practical lesson can you learn for your own life from the slaying of the Passover Lamb?

Passover lamb is the shadow of Jesus christ.
By shedding of His blood the Sinners get
redemption by believing in Him. I am
Saved by the blood of Jesus christ, By
Grace through faith. Praise the Lord.

LESSON 2

In the blank space in the right-hand margin write the letter of the correct answer.

11. The book of Leviticus is really
    a. a summary of the entire Mosaic Law
    b. a recapitulation of the chief events of the wilderness wan-
       derings of Israel
    c. a handbook of instruction for the priests of Israel
    d. a day-by-day account of certain events connected with the
       tribe of Levi taken from Moses' diary

 C

12. The five offerings demanded under the Mosaic Law
    a. portrayed different aspects of the death of Christ
    b. completely removed the guilt and stain of sin if the offerer
       followed the prescribed rituals and gave all five offerings at
       one time
    c. could be offered only by the priests since no provision was
       made in the Mosaic Law for the sins of the common people
    d. were invalid unless accompanied by a cash donation to help
       support the priests and maintain the Tabernacle

 A

13. The sins of the grumbling Israelites were climaxed at Kadesh
    Barnea where they
    a. threatened to kill Moses and Aaron
    b. refused to go forward, trusting in the Lord, and conquer
       Canaan
    c. provoked Moses so much that he smote the rock in anger
       and was barred by God from going on to Canaan
    d. committed acts of immorality with the women of Moab

 B

14. Of all the people (over twenty years of age) who came out of
    Egypt the only ones who went on into Canaan were
    a. Moses and Aaron
    b. Joshua and Caleb
    c. Phinehas and Miriam
    d. Korah, Dathan and Abiram

 B

15. The place where the Children of Israel camped before finally
    going on to Canaan was
    a. Kadesh Barnea
    b. Meribah
    c. Mount Hor
    d. the plains of Moab

 D (A)

16. The book of Deuteronomy was designed to
a. review the history of Israel and acquaint a new generation of Israelites with the Law
b. give Joshua detailed military instructions for his forthcoming campaigns in Canaan
c. redress certain grievances of the Israelites who were discriminated against by some of the earlier laws
d. repeal some of the earlier laws which had led to acts of dissent and rebellion on the part of the younger generation

_____A_____

17. The extermination of the Canaanites was
a. designed to gratify the blood-lust of some of the young radicals in the Israelite army
b. both a punishment on the Canaanites for their sins and a preventative measure to ensure the moral purity of Israel
c. the major blot on Joshua's otherwise illustrious military career
d. a terrible mistake resulting from a misinterpretation of certain statements in the Mosaic Law
e. in no way commanded by God or even hinted at in the Law of Moses

_____B_____

18. Joshua's military strategy in Canaan involved
a. driving a wedge into the heart of the country by conquering the key city of Jericho first
b. a sudden attack on the south of the country to overthrow an alliance of his foes
c. a campaign in the north to complete the subjugation of the country
d. all the above and in the order stated
e. all the above except that the north was subjugated before the south

19. The only tribe to get territory on both sides of the river Jordan was
a. Judah
b. Ephraim
c. Manasseh
d. Gad

_____C_____

20. Which of the following cities of Canaan did NOT become "cities of refuge" in Israel?

a. Kedesh
b. Jericho
c. Hebron
d. Shechem

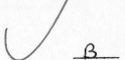

_B_

WHAT DO YOU SAY?

What practical lesson can you apply to your own life from studying the results of obedience and disobedience on the part of the Children of Israel?

If you obey the Lord, He will bless you and fulfill His promises to you. If you disobey the Lord you have to reap the consequences and also you will loose the blessings that are promised by God.

Lesson 3

We Want a King!

JUDGES

In the Book of Judges, we learn that Joshua's fears were well grounded. After his death, the nation repeatedly turned its back on God and went into idolatry. The Lord then allowed foreign armies to subdue the Israelites until the latter returned to Him in confession and forsaking of their sins. God then raised up a mighty military leader, known as a judge, to deliver the Jews from the oppressing nations. This deliverer would bring peace to the restless Israelites; then they would forget their lesson and lapse back into idolatry again.

The Book of Judges, of course, gets its name from those prominent leaders who became saviors of the nation at this critical time when there was no king in Israel and when everyone did that which was right in his own eyes. The repeated cycles of backslidings, subjugations and deliverances may be seen from the summary of the Book which appears on the next page. (The names of the more prominent judges are capitalized.)

Now with this background of the book, you will want to re-read the stories of such well-known names as Deborah, Gideon and Samson, and see more clearly how they fit into the history of the children of Israel: Deborah—with her amazing bravery as a commander-in-chief, and her never-to-be-forgotten song of victory. Gideon—with the much loved stories of his call and of his unparalleled success with an army of only 300, equipped with trumpets, lamps and pitchers. Samson—with the thrilling account of his great physical strength but the sad story of his moral weakness.

The Book of Judges closes with short sketches showing that the religious, moral and political state of the nation was at a very low ebb at this time.

Number of Israel's Back-slidings	Foreign Foes	Years of Oppression	Deliverer or Judge	Years of Peace	Scripture Reference
1	Mesopotamia	8	OTHNIEL	40	3:5-11
2	Moabites, Ammonites, Amalekites	18	EHUD	80	3:12-30
3	Philistines		Shamgar		3:31
4	Canaan	20	DEBORAH	40	4:2—5:31
5	Midian	7	GIDEON	40	6:1—8:35
6	(Civil War)	18	(Abimelech, a usurper.)	3	9:1-57
7	Unknown		Tola		10:1, 2
				45	
8	Unknown		Jair		10:3-5
9	Ammonites	18	JEPHTHAH	31	10:6—12:7
10	Unknown		Ibzan		12:8-10
11	Unknown		Elon		12:11, 12
12	Unknown		Abdon		12:13-15
13	Philistines	40	SAMSON	20	13:1—16:31

RUTH

The events in this book took place during the time of the Judges. Because of famine in Israel, a Jewish lady named Naomi went with her husband and two sons to Moab. One of her sons married a girl of Moab named Ruth. After Naomi's husband and two sons died, Ruth travelled back with her to Bethlehem.

It was a rule in Israel that when a husband died, a near relative should marry the widow in order to preserve the family name and to keep the property in the family. A very gracious Jew named Boaz, a relative of Ruth's former husband, signified his willingness to marry Ruth, and thus became what was known as her "kinsman redeemer."

Ruth bore a son named Obed, one of the ancestors of the Lord Jesus Christ. Thus Ruth, though a Gentile, is listed in the genealogy of the Savior (Matthew 1:5).

I SAMUEL

About 280 years after Joshua led the children of Israel into the promised land, they had reached a critical point in their history. Instead of being a blessing to the nation, the priesthood had utterly failed. The sons of Eli, the high priest, proved to be worthless, and the Israelites lacked spiritual leadership.

It is at this crisis hour that Samuel appears. God will now speak to His people through prophets,[1] rather than through the priesthood— first through Samuel, and then through others raised up by the Lord, some of whom were instructed in Samuel's schools.

In addition to the internal weakness of God's people, they were being troubled by the Philistine armies from without. They finally went to Samuel and demanded a king like the other nations. Up until now, the nation had been a theocracy—that means that God had been their Ruler. Now, in requesting a king, they were really rejecting God.

Samuel, therefore, was instructed to anoint Saul as king of Israel. At first this man's reign was promising, but he was not a true man of God, and so he lapsed into deeper and deeper sin. First, he served as a priest, a thing forbidden to anyone outside the family of Aaron. Second, he made an unnecessary vow that almost cost his son Jonathan's life. Third, he spared an enemy king named Agag when he had been ordered to slay him. Fourth, he killed some of the priests of Jehovah. Then, he made repeated, jealous attacks on the life of David, a young man who gained tremendous popularity by slaying Goliath, the Philistine giant. Finally, he went to a witch to seek guidance.

---

[1] A prophet is simply a spokesman for God who warns the people to turn from their sin, and often predicts exact events that will follow obedience and disobedience.

After his third mistake, God rejected him as king, and David was anointed in his place. However, David was not able to reign as king while Saul was alive, but rather spent years hiding from the latter's murderous attacks. Eventually Saul lost his army. Three of his sons were killed and he was doomed to fall into the hands of the Philistines. Rather than suffer this shame, he committed suicide.

II SAMUEL

The second Book of Samuel is devoted almost entirely to the reign of David. For seven and a half years after Saul's death, he ruled only over Judah. One of Saul's sons, Ishbosheth, had seized the reins of government over the northern tribes, and war broke out between the two sections of the kingdom. Finally, Ishbosheth was killed and David was anointed king over all the nation.

The early part of his reign was devoted to conquering Israel's enemies, notably the Philistines. He made Jerusalem the political and religious capital, and desired to build a temple for the Lord there: but God forbade this because David was a man of war. However, God promised him that his throne would last forever, and that he would always have descendants to sit upon the throne.

Chapter 11 records the sad story of his shameful sin. About one year later he repented when the prophet Nathan confronted him with his guilt; however, God disciplined him severely by troubles in his family:
1. The child born as a result of his sin died.
2. His son Amnon was killed by another son Absalom.
3. Absalom revolted and drove David into exile.

At last Absalom was killed and David returned to Jerusalem. At the close of his reign, he proudly took a census of Israel, boasting in its size and strength, rather than relying on the Lord. God sent a pestilence and destroyed 70,000 men. When David erected an altar and offered up sacrifices to God, the plague was stayed.

Take the Self-Check Test on page 3/5 and correct your answers. Exam questions for Lesson 3 will be found on pages 4/9-11.

HOW WELL ARE YOU DOING?

In the right-hand margin circle the following statements "True" or "False":

1. Joshua's fears for Israel were unfounded (p. 3/1).   T   (F)

2. The Judges were men raised up of God to deliver the Israelites from the captivities into which their sins had led them (p. 3/1).   (T)   F

3. Israel's first captivity, during the period covered by the book of Judges, was to the Moabites (p. 3/2).   T   (F)

4. One of the Judges was a woman (p. 3/1).   (T)   F

5. The story covered by the book of Ruth took place in the days of the Judges (p. 3/2).   (T)   F

6. The man who married Ruth when she arrived in Bethlehem became her kinsman redeemer (pp. 3/2, 3).   (T)   F

7. Samuel was a priest (p. 3/3).   T   (F)

8. Saul was rejected by God as being Israel's king after his third failure (p. 3/4).   (T)   F

9. David set up a rival kingdom to that of Saul and made Jerusalem the capital from which he warred against his rival (p. 3/4).   (T)   F

10. Because of his desire to build God a Temple, God told David that his dynasty would never end (p. 3/4).   T   (F)

Turn to the end of the book for the answers to these questions. Do NOT send them to the Correspondence School.

3/5

The Downfall of the Monarchy

I AND II KINGS

These books embrace a period of 453 years in the history of the kingdom. They begin with the death of David and the crowning of his son Solomon as king. The latter asked God for wisdom and was given not only wisdom, but riches and honor. Outstanding among his achievements was the building of a magnificent temple for the Lord and of a house for himself. But he erred in marrying heathen wives who lured him into idolatry. Also, he accumulated horses, and trusted in them rather than in the Lord.

When Solomon died, his son Rehoboam was next in line to succeed him. However, instead of decreasing the taxes which Solomon had levied to finance his luxurious reign, Rehoboam threatened to increase the people's burden. Thereupon, the northern ten tribes, known as Israel, revolted and named Jeroboam as king, with capital in Samaria. Rehoboam was left only with the tribe of Judah, and parts of Levi, Simeon and Benjamin. This is what is known as the divided kingdom; the ten tribes of Israel were the Northern Kingdom (also referred to as Ephraim), and Judah became the Southern Kingdom with headquarters at Jerusalem.

Then followed a series of kings in each kingdom, the kings of Israel being all bad, and those of Judah being both bad and good. The kingdom of Israel continued until it was taken into captivity by the Assyrians in 721 B.C. Judah continued for about 134 more years, then was taken captive by the Babylonians.

Several important points should be noted before leaving the subject of the divided kingdom.

1. Special emphasis is given to certain kings.
    a. Jeroboam, first king of Israel, who set up golden calves in Dan and Bethel as idols.
    b. Ahab, notoriously wicked king of Israel, husband of Jezebel, and worshipper of heathen god, Baal.
    c. The good kings of Judah—Asa, Jehoshaphat, Jehoash, Amaziah, Azariah, Jotham, Hezekiah and Josiah.

2. The prophets were active during this period; for instance, Elijah gained his great victory over the Baal-worshippers on Mt. Carmel during Ahab's reign. Then Elisha, famous for his many miracles, prophesied to the kings of Israel from Joram to Jehoahaz. Finally, many of the prophets whose words are recorded in the latter part of the Old Testament ministered during these years.

I AND II CHRONICLES

At first glance, these two books seem to be merely a repetition of portions of history that have been previously covered in the Old Testament. I Chronicles, for instance, is very much like I and II Samuel; it gives a fairly full account of David's reign. II Chronicles parallels I and II Kings in that it records the reign of Solomon and then reviews the kings of Judah under the divided kingdom.

And yet there are certain respects in which Chronicles are very different from the books that precede them.

1. I Chronicles opens with nine chapters of genealogies, beginning with Adam and continuing at least to the time that Judah was taken into captivity by the Babylonians (I Chronicles 6:15).
2. The Chronicles repeat the story from a religious and priestly standpoint rather than from a historical and political view. The ark, the

Levites, the priests, the porters and the temple itself are given prominence.

3. The Northern Kingdom, Israel, is practically unnoticed. It is the reign of David and his direct successors with whom God is interested because they are the line through which the Messiah was to come.
4. David's sin is largely passed over; rather the emphasis throughout is on the blessings that follow obedience.

In the last two verses of II Chronicles, we get a clue as to reasons for both these books. There we read of the decree of Cyrus[1] permitting the captives of Judah to return to Jerusalem after 70 years in exile. In other words, these books were written *after* the Babylonian captivity. In returning to their homeland, the Jewish people would require certain information.

1. They would need to know their genealogies in order to find out what portions of land belonged to them.
2. They would also need their genealogies to tell which ones were eligible to serve as priests and Levites in the temple.

In addition, the Books of Chronicles would give the returning exiles a spiritual outline of their past history, and best of all, it would brighten the hope of their coming Messiah, who would sit on the Throne of David.

EZRA

When Cyrus decreed that the Jewish exiles could return to their land and rebuild the temple, Zerubbabel assembled an expedition of 50,000 people and went to Jerusalem. They quickly went to work and laid the foundation of the temple, but they were soon hindered by some

---

[1] Cyrus was a king of Persia. The Jews were originally taken into captivity by the Babylonians. However, during their captivity, the Persians conquered the Babylonians, and thus Cyrus was in a position to release the captives.

Samaritans whose help had been refused. A considerable delay followed until the prophets, Haggai and Zechariah, encouraged the people to get on with the work.[1] Finally, in the reign of Darius, the building was completed and dedicated amid much rejoicing.

Approximately 60 years later, Ezra led another group of about 1700 exiles back to Jerusalem. Upon arrival, the leader was grieved to find that many of the people, even priests and princes, had married foreign wives. He then undertook the work of reform, with the result that the people confessed their sin and agreed to put away their heathen wives.

NEHEMIAH

Although the temple was now rebuilt, the walls of Jerusalem were in ruins, so that the city was subject to attack from foreign foes. During the reign of Artaxerxes, king of Persia, a Jew named Nehemiah was authorized to go back to Jerusalem and rebuild the city. Again the Samaritans opposed vigorously, but Nehemiah was not easily discouraged. He organized, armed and trained the people so well that the work was finished in 52 days. Then the people were assembled and the law was read to them. A revival broke out, with fasting, confession, forsaking of sins, and worship.

After twelve years in Jerusalem, Nehemiah returned to Persia. During his absence, the people lapsed into sin, so that when he came back to his native land again, he found them allowing strangers in the temple, failing to support the Levites, breaking the Sabbath and marrying foreign wives. Nehemiah reformed these abuses and instructed the people in the ways of the Lord.

At this point, the history of the Old Testament actually closes. These events took place approximately 400 years before the birth of Christ, and nothing is recorded in the Bible of the following four centuries. The last prophet of the Old Testament, Malachi, lived during the time of Nehemiah, so that his book is actually contemporary with this one.

---

[1] The writings of these prophets will be studied near the close of the Old Testament.

ESTHER

The thrill-packed story of Esther took place in the court of the Persian king sometime between the first and second return to Jerusalem under Zerubbabel and Ezra. In other words, it belongs between the sixth and seventh chapters of the book of Ezra.

It is an account of wonderful deliverance of the Jews from a clever plot by their enemy, Haman. Esther was a Jewish girl who became queen of Persia when King Ahasuerus became displeased with his wife, Vashti. Esther's cousin, Mordecai, was a godly Israelite who sat at the king's gate, and who at one time had revealed a plot against the king's life.

Because Mordecai would not bow to Haman, the latter was enraged and succeeded in persuading the king to sign and seal an edict calling for the destruction of all Jews on a certain date. Any such law of the Medes and Persians could not be reversed or changed under any circumstances.

In response to Mordecai's instructions, Esther risked her life by going before the king uninvited. She then asked the king and Haman to a banquet. Before the banquet took place, the king learned of Mordecai's unrewarded act in exposing the plot on his life, so Ahasuerus ordered Haman to proclaim publicly Mordecai as the man whom the king delighted to honor.

At the banquet, Esther, for the first time, revealed her nationality to the king, then told him of Haman's wicked trick to kill all Jews. The king quickly ordered Haman to be hanged on the gallows which he had prepared for Mordecai.

The next time Esther appeared before the king, she obtained permission for the Jews to defend themselves on the day planned for their execution. The king consented, with the result that their enemies were slain. This wonderful deliverance has been celebrated ever since that time by the annual Feast of Purim.

The book shows God's wonderful care of His people, even though His name is not mentioned in it.

When you are ready, take Self-Check Test 4 and then grade your answers.

Next complete Exam 2 by answering questions 11-20 on pages 4/12-14. (You should have already answered questions 1-10 as part of your study of lesson 3.)

SELF CHECK TEST 4

TRY THESE REVIEW QUESTIONS

In the right-hand margin circle the following statements "True" or "False":

1. The great sin of Solomon was that of building the Temple in Jerusalem, despite warnings that his son, not he, should build it (p. 4/1). T (F)

2. When the united kingdom of Israel was divided into two separate kingdoms, the ten tribes remained loyal to Rehoboam (p. 4/1) T (F)

3. All the kings of Israel, the northern kingdom, were bad (p. 4/1). (T) F

4. The nation of Judah outlasted the nation of Israel by about 134 years (p. 4/1). (T) F

5. The good kings of Judah were Asa, Jehoshaphat, Jehoash, Amaziah, Azariah, Jotham, Hezekiah and Josiah (p. 4/2). (T) F

6. The two cities set aside as centers of calf-worship by Jeroboam were in the extreme north and south of his kingdom (pp. 4/2, 3). (T) F

7. The books of Chronicles concentrate on the history of David and his successors (p. 4/3). (T) F

8. The books of Chronicles were written after the Babylonian captivity and reflect the sentiments of the priests rather than of the historian or politician (p. 4/4). (T) F

9. The first contingent of Jews returning to Palestine after the Babylonian captivity were led by Ezra (p. 4/4). ⨯(T) (F)

10. It took Nehemiah 52 weeks (i.e. a whole year) to rebuild the walls of Jerusalem (p. 4/5). T (F)

Turn to the end of the book for the answers to these questions. Do NOT send them to the Correspondence School.

SUMMARY OF THE BIBLE

Exam 2
Lessons 3, 4

Name _Elsie Mathews_ '
(print plainly)

Exam
Grade_____

Address_____

| | | Zip | Class |
| City_____ | State_____ | Code_____ | Number_____ |

Instructor _____

LESSON 3

In the blank space in the right-hand margin write the letter of the correct answer.

1. The Lord allowed foreign armies to repeatedly invade Israel after the death of Joshua because the Israelites
   a. were militarily weak and needed to learn the value of having a standing army
   b. turned away from God again and again to worship idols
   c. insisted on trusting in a political alliance with Egypt for protection rather than trusting in God
   d. expected their priests to lead them into battle thus violating the "separation of church and state" principle

_B___

2. The judges were
   a. military leaders raised up by God to deliver the Israelites from their enemies
   b. experts in the Mosaic law who presided in the Israelite law courts
   c. a group of travelling Levites (lawyers) who set up circuit courts to handle criminal cases in Israel
   d. drawn from the ranks of the priesthood, the only educated caste in Israel

_A___

3. How does God characterize the days of the Judges? He says that every man did
   a. what was right in the eyes of God
   b. what was right in the eyes of his neighbors
   c. what was right in his own eyes
   d. what was wrong in his own eyes

   _C_

4. The judge who delivered Israel from the Midianites was
   a. the judge who slew his enemies with the jaw-bone of an ass
   b. the son-in-law of Caleb
   c. strongly influenced by a woman, Deborah by name
   d. able to win his victory with a tiny army of three hundred men

   _D_

5. Ruth's kinsman-redeemer was Boaz. He assumed this position when he
   a. gave her his shoe to signify that he was walking in the ways of God
   b. married her to preserve the family name and the family inheritance
   c. became the father of Obed and thus an ancestor both of David and Jesus
   d. became the last of the judges and the first of the prophets

   _B_

6. The failure of the priesthood to provide true spiritual leadership climaxes in the days of Eli. The mark of this failure is seen in
   a. the drunkenness and immorality of Eli
   b. Eli's marriage to a pagan
   c. the fact that Eli was continually absent from Shiloh where the Tabernacle was located
   d. the wickedness of Eli's sons, Hophni and Phinehas

   _D_

7. With the choosing of Saul to be king of Israel, the nation passed from
   a. a theocracy to a monarchy
   b. a democracy to a monarchy
   c. a dependency to a democracy
   d. a dependency to a dictatorship

   _A_

8. Which of the following was NOT one of Saul's recorded sins? He
   a. intruded into the priest's office
   b. spared an enemy king God had commanded him to execute
   c. killed some of the priests of God
   d. accepted bribes from corrupt judges and politicians
   e. was insanely jealous of David and sought to have him killed
   f. consulted a witch

9. David was
   a. anointed king while Saul was still alive
   b. raised to the throne of Judah upon the death of Saul
   c. anointed king over all the Tribes after the death of Ishbo-sheth
   d. anointed king in three stages so all the above statements are correct

10. Which of the following did David NOT do? He
    a. subjugated the Philistines and Israel's other foes
    b. made Jerusalem the capital of Israel
    c. built a Temple to the Lord in Jerusalem
    d. sinned in a shameful way and with disastrous results
    e. took a census of Israel simply to glory in the size and strength of the nation

WHAT DO YOU SAY?

Which of the Judges impresses you most, and why?

Deborah: she was a bold, God fearing and God honoring woman leader. She stood for the Lord while all others were fallen and turned away from God. She was a chosen vessel for God.

LESSON 4

In the blank space in the right-hand margin write the letter of the correct answer.

11. Solomon's great sin was that of
   a. neglecting to build the Temple
   b. marrying a host of foreign wives
   c. making war against the Gibeonites who had been given political asylum in Israel
   d. setting up the brazen serpent, originally made by Moses, as an object of national veneration

12. The Twelve-tribed nation of Israel was divided into two separate kingdoms in the reign of Rehoboam. The incident which sparked the revolt of the Ten Tribes was Rehoboam's
   a. refusal to cut taxes and his threat to greatly increase them instead
   b. failure to win a decisive military victory over the Egyptians
   c. marriage to a woman of Judah rather than to a woman from one of the northern tribes
   d. decision to remove the capital from Jerusalem to Jericho

13. Which of the following is true?
   a. The nation of Israel in the north outlasted the nation of Judah in the south by about 134 years
   b. All the kings of Israel were good; some of the kings of Judah were good but most were bad
   c. The first king of the northern tribes (Israel) sinned against God by setting up golden calves as objects of worship
   d. The nations of Israel and Judah were both eventually taken into captivity by the Assyrians

14. Elijah prophesied during the reign of the king who
   a. was responsible for the division of the united kingdom of Israel into two rival nations
   b. "made Israel to sin" by setting up rival and idolatrous shrines in Dan and Bethel to prevent the northerners from going to Jerusalem to worship
   c. married Jezebel the notoriously wicked woman who worshipped the heathen god Baal
   d. entered into an alliance with the Assyrians and introduced idolatrous forms of worship into the nation of Judah

15. The books of Chronicles

    a. are a repetition of the books of Kings and create a problem to scholars because of the serious differences between them and the books of Kings

    b. were written mostly from the viewpoint of the prophets and discuss the affairs of the northern kingdom of Israel rather than the affairs of the much smaller kingdom of Judah

    c. concentrate mostly on the history of the Messianic line through David

    d. were written in the dark days just prior to the fall of Jerusalem and the Babylonian captivity and were intended to keep hope alive in the heart of the captive Jews

    C

16. The prophets who greatly encouraged the remnant, returned from the Babylonian captivity, in their efforts to rebuild the Temple were

    a. Ezra and Nehemiah

    b. Ezekiel and Daniel

    c. Haggai and Zechariah

    d. Micah and Malachi

    C

17. The Jews returned from the Babylonian captivity in three stages. The first contingent was led by

    a. Ezra

    b. Joshua

    c. Nehemiah

    d. Zerubbabel

    D

18. Nehemiah was commissioned by Artaxerxes to

    a. rebuild the Temple in Jerusalem

    b. repair the walls of Jerusalem

    c. restore the throne of David in Jerusalem

    d. revive the religion of Judaism in Jerusalem

    B

19. Which of the following books are contemporaneous?

    a. Daniel and Esther

    b. Ezra and Ezekiel

    c. Nehemiah and Malachi

    d. Job and Ezra

    C

20. Esther was a Jewish girl who
   a. married Artaxerxes the Persian king and persuaded him to restore the Jews to their homeland
   b. brought about the promotion of Haman which made it possible for him to plan the extermination of the Jews
   c. influenced Ahasuerus to punish Haman and protect the Jews from the hatred of their foes
   d. introduced Mordecai to Ahasuerus with the result that Mordecai was able to save the king's life from an assassination plot promoted by Haman

   ✓ ___c___

WHAT DO YOU SAY?

Esther made her life count for God. Describe one way in which you have made yours count for God.

I am trying to follow the truths of the Bible. Stand for my Faith. I trust in the Lord and depend upon His promises during the trials in my life. I believe that He is able — Nothing is too difficult for my Lord.

"Give Me Thy Heart"

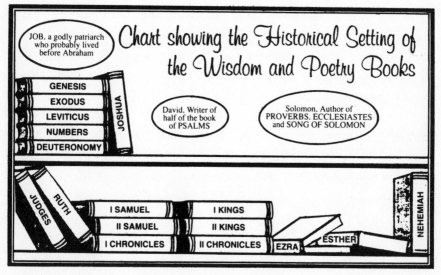

Chart showing the Historical Setting of the Wisdom and Poetry Books

In the above chart, an attempt has been made to:

1. Arrange the historical books (Genesis through Esther) in the order in which the events actually occurred. Thus you will notice that:
    a. Ruth is shown as having lived during the time of the Judges.
    b. I Chronicles covers approximately the same time period as I and II Samuel.
    c. II Chronicles covers approximately the same time period as I and II Kings.
    d. The events in the Book of Esther occurred during the interval between the sixth and seventh chapters of Ezra.
2. Indicate the time when the authors of the Wisdom and Poetry books lived and wrote.

JOB

Job probably lived around the time of Abraham. He was a wealthy and righteous man whom God allowed to be severely tested by Satan by being stripped of possessions and family, and finally by being afflicted with a painful and loathsome disease. Three friends who came to comfort him were so astonished when they saw his pitiful condition that they could not speak for seven days. Then they reasoned with him at great length that the righteous do not suffer, and that therefore he must have sinned very greatly. Job continually protested his innocence, accused them of being unmerciful, and blamed God for all his troubles. A young man named Elihu then appeared and spoke for God. He criticized Job's three friends for their failure to help Job, then reproved the latter for finding fault with God's dealings. At last, Job got a sight of the greatness, righteousness, power, and wisdom of God, and he repented of his sin. When he prayed for his friends, his troubles ended, and the Lord gave him twice as many possessions as he had before.

PSALMS

This is one of the most loved books in the Bible. It is a collection of poems or hymns expressing in marvelous language the emotions and experiences of God's people. David is believed to have written at least 73 of the Psalms; Moses, Asaph, and Solomon wrote some; and the authors of 50 others are unknown. Many of these poems have a definite historical background; that is, they were composed to describe some experience through which the nation of Israel, or some individual was passing. Then, many Psalms are clearly prophetic in that they describe the coming of Christ in His suffering and in His glory, or they tell of the future of Israel. Finally, it should be said that the Psalms are filled with practical instruction for God's people. In the original language of the Old Testament, the Psalms were divided into five books, as follows: Book I—Psalms 1-41; Book II—Psalms 42-72; Book III—Psalms 73-89; Book IV—Psalms 90-106; Book V—Psalms 107-150.

PROVERBS

This book is a collection of wise sayings, written for the most part by King Solomon. Someone has well named them, "Laws from heaven for life on earth." There are warnings against sin of all kinds—unchastity, idleness, falsehood, adultery, pride, injustice; there are instructions for parents and for children, for husbands and for wives, for rich and poor. Here Wisdom speaks to all who will listen, offering priceless advice on how to live a clean, honest, upright life, avoiding the heartache, disgrace and pain of sin.

ECCLESIASTES

Here is told the unsuccessful quest of a man[1] for happiness on earth apart from God. It seems that this man tried everything in his search for the greatest good—science, philosophy, pleasure, building, wealth, music, and even human religion. But he was bitterly disappointed, and concluded that all was vanity under the sun. The key phrase of the book is "under the sun"—meaning that it tells of a life as seen from the earthly, human viewpoint, not from "above the sun" which is God's view. Failure to recognize this fact has led to some erroneous uses of this book. The lesson of Ecclesiastes is that the human heart cannot be satisfied apart from the Lord, and the book was written so that "others might be spared the anguish and disappointment of treading the same weary path."

SONG OF SOLOMON

This tender love story is a gem of literature. It is called the Song of Songs in order to indicate its superiority to other songs. There are two principal ideas as to the plot of the book and its interpretation.

Perhaps the most common view is that it describes the genuine

---

[1] Solomon is generally considered to be the author.

affection between Solomon and a Shulamite maiden. He woos and wins her from her home in Shunem, and brings her to his palace in Jerusalem. The interpretation is that the love of Solomon is a type of Jehovah's love for the faithful remnant of Israel. Then it can also be applied to Christ's love for the church.

Another view sees three principal characters in the story—Solomon, the maiden and her shepherd-lover. Solomon, the man with a thousand wives, seeks to win the heart of this maiden, even bringing her to his royal palace. But she remains true to her own lover. When Solomon flatters her, she only replies by describing her own beloved. She is thus a picture of the faithful remnant of Israel which remains true to Jehovah in spite of the allurements of the world. Finally, her shepherd-lover appears and takes his bride back to his home.[1]

---

[1] Whichever interpretation one prefers, it is helpful to mark in the Bible the persons who are speaking in the various portions of the book, as follows:

The Maiden—ch. 1:1-7, 12-14, 16, 17. ch. 2:1, 3-17. ch. 3:1-4, ch. 4:16. ch. 5:2-8, 10-16. ch. 6:2, 3, 13 (last two clauses). ch. 7:9b-13. ch. 8:1-4, 6, 7, 10-12, 14.

Solomon—ch. 1:8-11, 15. ch. 2:2. ch. 3:5. ch. 4:1-15. ch. 5:1. ch. 6:4-12. ch. 7:1-9a (ending "like the best wine"). ch. 8:13.

Companions—ch. 3:6-11. ch. 5:9. ch. 6:1, 13a. ch. 8:5, 8, 9.

from BIBLE HANDBOOK by Walter Scott

When you have mastered this lesson, take the Self-Check Test on page 5/5. Look up the answers to this test and see how well you did.

Then take the first part of Exam 3 (covering lesson 5), questions 1-10 on pages 6/7-9 (right after lesson 6).

HOW MUCH CAN YOU REMEMBER?

In the right-hand margin circle the following statements "True" or "False":

1. The events in the book of Esther may be inserted chronologically, between the 6th and 7th chapters of Ezra (p. 5/1). (T) F

2. Job probably lived about ·the same time as Moses (p. 5/2). T (F)

3. Right from the start, Job seemed to recognize, instinctively, that Satan was to blame for all his troubles (p. 5/2). T (F)

4. David, Moses, Asaph and Solomon all contributed to the writing of the Psalms (p. 5/2). (T) F

5. Psalm 90 begins the fourth book of the Psalms (p. 5/2). (T) F

6. The book of Proverbs warns against sin of all sorts (p. 5/3). (T) F

7. Solomon wrote all, or part at least, of three books of the Bible (pp. 5/3, 4). (T) F

8. The only thing "under the sun" in which Solomon found lasting happiness was in music (p. 5/3). T (F)

9. The Song of Solomon is a love story (p. 5/3). (T) F

10. The most common view of the Song of Solomon depicts, Solomon as a type of the world seeking to allure into its embrace the believer who has given himself to the Lord (pp. 5/3, 4). T (F)

Turn to the end of the book for the answers to these questions. Do NOT send them to the Correspondence School.

The Major Prophets

In completing lessons 6 through 8, the student should refer to the "Chart of the Kings and Prophets of Israel and Judah" on page 6/2. There he will see at a glance the approximate time at which each of the prophets ministered. In the lessons on the prophets, key words or phrases are capitalized.

ISAIAH

This great prophet's ministry extended from the last year of the reign of Uzziah (also called Azariah) to the end of Hezekiah's reign. It was during this very period that the Northern Kingdom, Israel, was carried away by Assyria. Judah, too, was being threatened by the Assyrians, but God miraculously delivered them from this foe.

Although Isaiah prophesied at times to Israel before her captivity, his message for the most part was addressed to the people of Judah. He thundered out against their many sins—particularly the sin of IDOLATRY, and warned them that they would be taken captive by Babylonia as a result.

Isaiah also wrote of God's judgment on the nations that were enemies of His people, primarily ASSYRIA and BABYLONIA, but also Moab, Damascus, Egypt and Tyre.

Finally, amid all his messages of denouncement and doom, he has a wonderful message of COMFORT as he describes the coming Messiah

Judah	Prophets	Israel	World Powers
Rehoboam		Jeroboam	
Abijam			
Asa			
		Nadab	
		Baasha	
		Elah	
		Zimri	
		Omri	
Jehoshaphat	Elijah	Ahab	
			Syria
	Elisha	Ahaziah	
Jehoram		Jehoram	
Ahaziah		Jehu	
Athaliah			
Jehoash	Joel	Jehoahaz	
		Jehoash	
Amaziah	Jonah	Jeroboam II	
Uzziah	Amos		Assyria
		Zechariah	
		Shallum	
Jotham	Hosea	Menahem	
		Pekahiah	
Ahaz		Pekah	
Hezekiah	Micah ISAIAH	Hoshea	
		ASSYRIAN CAPTIVITY 722 B.C.	
Manasseh			Thebes destroyed
	Nahum		
Amon			Assyria overthrown 612 B.C.
Josiah	Zephaniah Habakkuk		
Jehoahaz	JEREMIAH		1st Babylonian invasion
Jehoiakim	Obadiah		
Jehoiachin			2nd invasion
Zedekiah			
	EZEKIEL		3rd invasion
BABYLONIAN CAPTIVITY 586 B.C.	DANIEL		Persia
			Cyrus
Zerubbabel			Darius I
	Haggai Zechariah		
			Xerxes
Ezra			
Nehemiah			Darius II
	Malachi		

—the only Hope of the nation. He foretells Christ's birth, life, suffering, death, resurrection and His still future glorious reign on earth. It is because of these wonderful passages about the Lord Jesus, written about 700 years before His birth, that we speak of Isaiah as the EVANGELICAL PROPHET.

JEREMIAH and LAMENTATIONS

Jeremiah is best known as the WEEPING prophet. This is the key to his writings, for if we remember this and the reason for his weeping, we shall be able to understand his message.

Jeremiah began his ministry to Judah during the reign of Josiah. This was after Israel had fallen to the Assyrians, and not many years before the end of the kingdom of Judah.

God revealed to the prophet that Judah's sins would result in that nation's being taken into CAPTIVITY by the BABYLONIANS and held in exile for seventy years. Jeremiah's sorrowful mission was to announce this fact to his fellow-countrymen, and to advise them to SUBMIT to the Babylonian power. They accused him of being a traitor and made an attack on his life.

When Jerusalem finally fell to the foreign invaders, Jeremiah was one of those who was permitted to stay in the homeland, while the bulk of the nation was carried away. He now advised the remaining people not to flee to EGYPT for help, but they disregarded his counsel, and carried him off with them. There the prophet died.

Actually, the FALL OF JERUSALEM was a time of terrible suffering and anguish. It was this fearful catastrophe that brought forth the Book of LAMENTATIONS—a series of tearful laments over the desolation of the city, wrung from the heart of the prophet.

In addition to predicting the Babylonian captivity, Jeremiah also foresaw the destruction of that empire at the end of seventy years and the return of the Jews to their land.

EZEKIEL

This prophet, commonly addressed as SON OF MAN, was taken to

Babylonia with the second group of captives, eleven years before Jerusalem was destroyed. He ministered to his fellow-exiles during the first twenty-seven years of the captivity. They falsely expected to return to Jerusalem soon, but he taught them that they must first return to the Lord.

His prophecy is divided into three parts. First, he rehearses the sins of Judah, and warns of God's impending judgment in the captivity of the people and the destruction of the capital. This is all vividly announced in unusual visions and symbolic acts. A bright, shining cloud, figure of God's presence, is seen lingering over the temple; then reluctantly departing. This meant that God could no longer dwell among His people because of their sin, and His sword of judgment must soon descend on the polluted temple.

In the second section, Judah's neighbors are condemned because of their idolatry and their cruel treatment of God's people. These are the Ammonites, Moabites, Edomites, the Philistines, TYRE, SIDON and EGYPT.

Finally, in the last portion, Ezekiel tells of the RESTORATION and REUNION of the entire nation, both Israel and Judah. When the people REPENT of their sins, God will put His HOLY SPIRIT within them. The Messiah will come to His people and destroy their last enemies. The TEMPLE will be rebuilt, and the GLORY OF THE LORD will return to it. These prophecies have not yet been fulfilled, but look forward to Christ's one thousand year reign on earth, the Millennium.

DANIEL

Among the first group of Jews taken into exile by the Babylonians was a young lad named Daniel. He soon arose to a position of prominence in the palace of the king, Nebuchadnezzar. There in the midst of immorality and idolatry, Daniel was characterized by uncompromising purity and fearless devotion to God.

During Nebuchadnezzar's reign Daniel foretold that there would be four successive GENTILE WORLD POWERS, namely BABYLONIA, MEDO-PERSIA, GREECE and ROME. At the end of the TIMES OF

THE GENTILES, God would set up His KINGDOM on earth—one that would last forever.

Daniel continued to serve in the Babylonian court up to and including the time of Belshazzar. To that king, he solemnly announced that the Babylonian empire was finished, and that the Medes and Persians would now seize the reins of world government.

Darius was one of the early Medo-Persian rulers over conquered Babylonia and it was during his reign that Daniel was cast into the den of lions. However, the prophet's loyalty to God won him divine preservation and a place of leadership in this kingdom also. In his vision of seventy "weeks" (490 years), Daniel predicted the time that would elapse until the crucifixion of Christ, then told of a still future period of GREAT TRIBULATION for the Jews before Christ sets up His Throne.

The last mention of Daniel is during the reign of Cyrus. It was this Persian king who decreed that the Jews could return to their land. Thus Daniel lived through the entire seventy-year captivity of JUDAH. His closing prophecies deal with the time of the end when ANTICHRIST will arise, when Israel's enemies will make their final assault, and when Christ will come to put down His foes and reign at Jerusalem over his restored people.

When you are ready, take Self-Check Test 6 and then grade your answers.

Next complete Exam 3 by answering questions 11-20 on pages 6/9-11. (You should have already answered questions 1-10 as part of your study of lesson 5.)

SELF CHECK TEST 6

REVIEW YOUR LESSON

In the right-hand margin circle the following statements "True" or "False":

1. Isaiah and Jeremiah were contemporaries (p. 6/2).　　　T　**F**

2. Isaiah prophesied solely to the northern kingdom of Israel (p. 6/1).　　　**T**　F

3. Isaiah, because of his magnificent prophecies about the Lord Jesus, is called "the evangelical prophet" (p. 6/3).　　　**T**　F

4. Jeremiah was accused by his countrymen of being a traitor because of his loyalty to the truth of God much of which was unwelcome news to his fellows (p. 6/3).　　　**T**　F

5. When Jeremiah's prophecies concerning the coming of the Babylonians finally came to pass in the most dreadful literal way, his countrymen acknowledged him as a prophet and thereafter heeded his advice (p. 6/3).　　　T　**F**

6. The prophet commonly addressed in his book as "son of man" is Ezekiel (p. 6/3).　　　**T**　F

7. The second section of Ezekiel's prophecy is mostly concerned with judgments pronounced against Judah's neighboring Gentile states (p. 6/4).　　　**T**　F

8. The one great theme of prophecy conspicuously absent from Ezekiel is that of the Millennium (p. 6/4).　　　T　**F**

9. Daniel lived in exile in Babylon from the time of Nebuchadnezzar to the time of the Persian king Cyrus (pp. 6/4, 5).　　　**T**　F

10. Daniel was cast into the den of lions by Nebuchadnezzar (p. 6/5).　　　T　**F**

Turn to the end of the book for the answers to these questions. Do NOT send them to the Correspondence School.

SUMMARY OF THE BIBLE

Exam 3
Lessons 5, 6

Name_____*Elsie Matthews*_____
(print plainly)

Exam
Grade_____

Address_____

City_____State_____Zip Code_____Class Number_____

Instructor_____

LESSON 5

In the blank space in the right-hand margin write the letter of the correct answer.

1. In all probability, Job lived about the time of
   a. Enoch
   b. Abraham
   c. Moses
   d. Jonah

   _*B*_

2. Job's friends
   a. sympathized with him in his troubles and encouraged him in his trust in God
   b. told Job he must be a very great sinner otherwise he would not be suffering so much
   c. helped Job see that Satan was the actual instigator of his troubles
   d. advised Job to become an atheist since his sufferings proved that God either did not exist or, if He did He could not be a God of love to allow Job to suffer so much

   _*B*_

3. Job's reaction to his troubles was to
   a. curse God and his friends
   b. confess at once that he had sinned and deserved to suffer
   c. promise God not to sin again if God would only restore him to his former health and happiness
   d. protest his innocence and blame God for what had happened to him

   _*D*_

4. God gave Job twice as much as he had before his sufferings began when Job finally repented and
   a. listened, without argument, to the speech of Elihu the mediator
   b. prayed for the people who had been criticizing him
   c. made a costly sacrifice at the altar
   d. put on sackcloth and ashes

B

5. The *entire* book of Psalms was written
   a. by David "the sweet singer of Israel"
   b. over a considerable period of time
   c. to commemorate definite historical events
   d. specifically for use by the Temple choir

B
C

6. Which of the following would NOT be true of the book of Psalms? It
   a. expresses the emotions and experiences of God's people
   b. is filled with practical instruction for the people of God
   c. is one of the least read of the books of the Bible
   d. contains many prophecies about the two comings of Christ
   e. was divided into five books in the original Hebrew text of the Bible

C

7. "Laws from heaven for life on earth" sums up the book of
   a. Job
   b. Psalms
   c. Proverbs
   d. Ecclesiastes
   e. Song of Solomon

C

8. According to Ecclesiastes, in his desperate search for happiness, Solomon left out
   a. the findings of science
   b. the speculations of philosophy
   c. the possibilities of pleasure
   d. the knowledge of God
   e. the accumulation of money
   f. the practice of religion

D

9. Solomon found that everything "under the sun" was
  a. beautiful
  b. vain
  c. satisfying
  d. evil
  e. all the above

_b

10. According to the most popular view, the Song of Solomon
  a. has to do with an attempt, on the part of Solomon, to win to himself a young woman who, despite his flatteries and promises, remains true to her shepherd-fiancee
  b. depicts the faithful remnant of Israel remaining true to Jehovah despite the allurements of the world
  c. describes Solomon's love for a Shulamite woman who he successfully wins for his bride
  d. the attempt of a country girl to win the love of Solomon and be exalted to share his throne

C

B

WHAT DO YOU SAY?

Which of the five poetical books has been the greatest blessing in your life? Describe why or how.

Psalms - It gives me Comfort when I am desperate.
It enables me to give Praises and worship to the Lord.
I memmorise many of the Psalms in my young age.
It helps me throughout my life

LESSON 6

In the blank space in the right-hand margin write the letter of the correct answer.

11. The great foreign power which dominated the international scene during the days of Isaiah was
  a. Egypt
  b. Assyria
  c. Babylon
  d. Persia

_b_

12. Isaiah prophesied
a. to Israel alone warning her of imminent judgment because of her idolatry
b. to both Israel and Judah as well as announcing doom on various Gentile nations
c. solely of judgment with never a word of comfort to relieve the gloom of his predictions
d. about the same time as Jeremiah

 B

13. Which of the following best describes Jeremiah? He was the
a. evangelical prophet
b. the popular prophet
c. the alien prophet
d. the weeping prophet

 D

14. Jeremiah foretold the
a. overthrow of Nineveh
b. rejection of Israel as God's channel of blessing and the bringing in of the Church to take her place
c. the seventy-year captivity of the Jews in Babylon
d. the invasion of Israel in the last days by "Gog and Magog" (i.e. Russia) and her satellites

 C

15. The book of Lamentations was inspired by the fall of
a. Samaria
b. Jerusalem
c. Babylon
d. all the above

 B

16. The departure of the Shekinah glory cloud from Jerusalem was described by
a. Isaiah
b. Jeremiah
c. Ezekiel
d. Daniel

 C

17. The great theme in the third part of Ezekiel's prophecy is
a. the sins of Judah which make inevitable the destruction of the Temple and the captivity of the people
b. the restoration of Israel and Judah as one nation at the end times and the glories of the millennial kingdom
c. the fate of the Babylonians at the hands of the Persians
d. the doom of Judah's cruel Gentile neighbors

 B

18. Which of the following prophets ministered from exile in Babylonia?

a. Jeremiah and Ezekiel
b. Ezekiel and Daniel
c. Daniel and Jeremiah
d. Jeremiah, Ezekiel and Daniel

19. Which four world powers were subjects of Daniel's visions?

a. Egypt, Assyria, Babylon and Persia
b. Assyria, Babylon, Persia and Greece
c. Babylon, Persia, Greece and ·Rome
d. Persia, Greece, Rome and Carthage

20. Daniel foretold

a. the fall of Babylon and the seizure of the kingdom by the Medes and Persians
b. the time when the crucifixion of Christ would take place
c. the coming on the scene at the end times of the Antichrist
d. all the above

WHAT DO YOU SAY?

Read the first six chapters of Daniel. State what impresses you most about the personal life of Daniel and his three friends.

Daniel and his 3 friends stood firm for their Faith in. Their determination of "do not defile themselves" they kept. Their Faith in God and their prayer was wonderful. God almighty honoured their faith and faithfulness

The Minor Prophets

HOSEA

While Isaiah was prophesying in Judah, Hosea was active as a prophet in Israel. He began his ministry in the reign of Jeroboam II, and continued until after the nation had been captured by the Assyrians—one of the darkest periods in Jewish history.

It is easy to remember Hosea as the prophet with the UNFAITHFUL WIFE. God commanded him to marry a harlot named Gomer. True to her character, she left him to live shamefully in sin. Then God instructed His servant to buy her on the public market and bring her back in blessing.

The purpose of all this, of course, was to picture God's relationship with Israel. The nation had proved unfaithful, living in IDOLATRY and moral wickedness. For many years it would be without a king, a sacrifice or idols. That is its present status. Then when Israel will RETURN to the Lord in REPENTANCE, He will have mercy, EPHRAIM will then be forever cured of its idolatrous BACKSLIDING, and converted to God. Ephraim was the largest tribe of Israel, and the leader in rebellion. Hosea uses this name to include the entire ten tribes of Israel.

The book is a wonderful record of God's unfailing LOVE for His failing people.

JOEL

It is generally agreed that Joel prophesied to Judah from the reign of Joash to that of Ahaz. This would mean he was the first of the writing prophets.

He described a terrible PLAGUE OF LOCUSTS which devastated the entire land. By this vivid picture, the prophet vainly sought to call his people to repentance lest God should allow their foreign foes to invade the country.

However, his prophecy will have a future fulfillment in the DAY OF THE LORD, a time of great judgment preceded by terrible signs and wonders but followed by divine blessing.

Joel predicted the pouring out of the Spirit upon all flesh. The Day of PENTECOST was a pledge of this, but it will have its final fulfillment at the time of the restoration of Israel.

AMOS

This herdsman of Tekoa was a prophet to Israel during the reign of Jeroboam II. He was sent to preach at BETHEL—where a golden calf had been set up as an object of worship by Jeroboam I, first king of Israel.

As long as Amos confined his ministry to announcing God's judgment on Damascus, Gaza, Tyrus, Edom, Ammon and Moab, he was well received. However, when he turned to Judah and Israel and told of STERNER PUNISHMENT because of GREATER PRIVILEGE, he met opposition.

By a series of VISIONS, he pictured the imminence and certainty of God's wrath on Israel. However, the Lord would spare a REMNANT of the nation, he predicted, and eventually Israel would be restored and converted.

OBADIAH

It is not possible to state definitely when Obadiah lived. Some believe he was contemporary with Hosea, Joel and Amos; others feel he lived during the captivity.

The key word of this book is EDOM, for in it the prophet rebukes this nation for its unbrotherly spirit toward the Jews.

The Edomites were descendants of Esau, thus related to the Israelites. However, they refused passage through their country when Israel was marching from Egypt to Canaan. Years later, when the Babylonians destroyed Jerusalem, the Edomites showed their spite by joining in the massacre and plunder.

Because of their PRIDE and CRUELTY, Obadiah prophesies their UTTER DESTRUCTION. The Jewish people will be God's instrument to accomplish Edom's downfall. Then Israel will be delivered and will POSSESS all the land originally promised to them, including Edom.

JONAH

It is believed that Jonah prophesied to Israel during the reigns of Jehoahaz, Joash and Jeroboam II. However, the exact dates are not known.

God sent him to NINEVEH to cry out against its wickedness. This was the capital of ASSYRIA, Israel's great foe. Jonah feared that Nineveh might repent and be spared by God, so he fled toward Tarshish. Overtaken by a great storm, he was cast into the sea by his endangered shipmates, swallowed by a great fish, then cast out on dry land.

After this, Jonah willingly went to Nineveh and predicted that it would be destroyed in forty days. The city REPENTED at his preaching and God spared it for about 150 more years.

Jonah was angry that Nineveh escaped until God showed him that He has the right to show mercy to whomever He will.

Jonah's experience in the fish's belly is typical of (1) Christ's death, burial and resurrection, and (2) Israel's rejection, burial among the nations, and eventual restoration.

MICAH

The prophet's voice was heard in the days of Jotham, Ahaz and

Hezekiah, at about the same time as Isaiah.

He addressed the PEOPLE and RULERS OF SAMARIA and JERU-SALEM (capitals of Israel and Judah). Because of their idolatry, injustice and greed, these cities were doomed to destruction, the former by the ASSYRIANS, and the latter by the BABYLONIANS.

However, out of a third city, BETHLEHEM, Messiah will come and reign in Zion over a spared remnant of His people. He will crush the ASSYRIANS, and bring PEACE to Israel. In that day, the remnant will say, "Who is a God like unto Thee."

When you have mastered this lesson, take the Self-Check Test on page 7/5. Look up the answers to this test and see how well you did.

Then take the first part of Exam 4 (covering lesson 7), questions 1-10 on pages 8/7-10 (right after lesson 8).

SELF CHECK TEST 7

CHECK UP ON YOURSELF AGAIN

In the right-hand margin circle the following statements "True" or "False":

1. Hosea and Isaiah were contemporaries (p. 7/1).   (T)   F

2. Hosea warned Israel that idolatry was actually unfaithfulness to Jehovah (p. 7/1).   (T)   F

3. The present status of the nation of Israel as being free from idolatry but also without king or sacrifice was clearly seen by Hosea (p. 7/1).   (T)   F

4. The first of the writing prophets was Amos (p. 7/2).   T   (F)

5. Joel's occupation before God called him to be a prophet was that of a herdsman (p. 7/2).   T   (F)

6. Amos was sent to prophesy at Bethel where there was an ancient idolatrous center of calf-worship in Israel (p. 7/2).   (T)   F

7. Amos was given a series of visions to help him convey to the people the message that God had for them (p. 7/2).   (T)   F

8. The Edomites were the primary target of Obadiah's prophecy (p. 7/3).   (T)   F

9. The repentance of the Ninevites under the preaching of Jonah gave that city a respite of one and a half centuries before God finally overthrew their city (p. 7/3).   (T)   F

10. Micah prophesied to both Israel and Judah and foretold that both their capital cities would be destroyed (p. 7/4).   (T)   F

Turn to the end of the book for the answers to these questions. Do NOT send them to the Correspondence School.

More Minor Prophets

NAHUM

While the exact date of Nahum's prophecy is unknown, it is fairly certain that he ministered sometime between the fall of the Northern Kingdom and the destruction of Assyria.

His was a message of CONSOLATION to Judah. At a time when the Southern tribes were being threatened by the Assyrians, Nahum predicted not only that the enemy would be unsuccessful in taking Jerusalem, but that Nineveh would be utterly destroyed and never rebuilt. The battle against the capital of Assyria is described in great detail, including the overflow of the river and the devouring fire. Nahum looks upon Nineveh's ruin as God's JUST RETRIBUTION on a wicked people.

HABAKKUK

Habakkuk wrote his grand prophecy to JUDAH sometime before the Babylonian captivity, probably during the reign of Josiah.

There were two great questions on his mind. First, WHY did God fail to punish the sins of Judah? God's answer was that He would soon act in judgment by sending the BABYLONIANS to chastise His people.

But then Habakkuk was more distressed. WHY should God punish

Judah by a nation that was even more sinful? God replied that THE JUST SHALL LIVE BY FAITH; in other words, those who really trusted in the Lord would be saved, while all unbelievers, including the ruthless Babylonian people themselves, would eventually be destroyed.

These answers satisfied the prophet, so he closed with a prayer extolling God's majesty, and expressing trust in Him for the future.

ZEPHANIAH

The prophet tells us that he ministered in the days of Josiah, king of JUDAH.

There are two main themes of the book: God's JUDGMENT and His JOY. First, Zephaniah tells of JUDAH's coming doom because of its idolatry. The DAY OF THE LORD will be a time of great wrath, trouble and distress. A remnant is exhorted to repent so that they will be hidden from Jehovah's anger. Surrounding nations will also be punished for their wickedness, namely, Philistia, Moab, Ammon, Ethiopia and Assyria. Indeed, the day of the Lord will mean UNIVERSAL JUDGMENT. No wicked person will escape.

But Zephaniah also tells of Jehovah's joy in His restored people. Christ will return to earth in glory. The Jews will be gathered from captivity and will be a praise in the earth. When they are thus restored, God will rejoice over them with singing.

HAGGAI

Among the first captives to return to Jerusalem after the seventy-year exile was the prophet Haggai. Under Zerubbabel's leadership, a group of Jews had journeyed back from Babylon and began to REBUILD THE TEMPLE.

The Samaritan inhabitants vigorously opposed this project with the result that the work was suspended for awhile. Then the prophets, Haggai and Zechariah, arose to ENCOURAGE completion of the temple.

In his short prophecy, Haggai:
1. REBUKES the people for allowing the temple to remain in ruins while they lived in fine homes.
2. Tells them TO CONSIDER THEIR WAYS and to build the house of the Lord, for THE LORD WAS WITH THEM.
3. Reminds them of their past disobedience in this respect and of God's judgments upon them.
4. ENCOURAGES them that the Lord (the Desire of Nations) will come to the temple, and that its future glory will be greater than its past.
5. PREDICTS that Jehovah will overturn the kingdoms of the earth, but will save His chosen ones.

ZECHARIAH

Also a prophet to the returned captives, Zechariah joined with Haggai in ENCOURAGING the people to complete the REBUILDING OF THE TEMPLE.

In eight visions, using highly symbolic language, he predicted the overthrow of the Gentile world empires, the judgment of apostate Judaism because of their rejection of Christ, the CLEANSING, RESTORATION and GLORY of a remnant, and the future prosperity of Jerusalem.

Zechariah tells us more about the MESSIAH than any other minor prophet. He prophesies His entry into Jerusalem, His betrayal for thirty pieces of silver, His wounds, His death as the smitten SHEPHERD, His coming again to the Mount of Olives, and His millennial reign as High Priest and King. He also speaks of the Lord as the BRANCH and God's SERVANT.

Zechariah's picture of coming glory was designed to stimulate the temple builders to renewed endeavor.

MALACHI

The last prophet of the Old Testament was probably active during the closing part of Nehemiah's governorship. This was about 400 years before Christ. The moral condition of the people was at an extremely low level. In the Book of Malachi, we find God tenderly reasoning with the people while they dispute with Him and justify their own condition.

Among the abuses of Malachi's day were:

1. The people displayed a lack of love for the Lord.
2. The priests offered sacrifices that were imperfect.
3. They refused to do anything without pay.
4. The men of Judah were marrying idolatrous wives.
5. They neglected to pay their tithes.

Malachi foresees the coming of Christ, preceded by His MESSENGER, John the Baptist. Still later, he predicts the Day of the Lord when the Sun of Righteousness will arise in judgment on the ungodly, but in blessing on the faithful REMNANT who fear the Lord.

When you are ready, take Self-Check Test 8 and then grade your answers.

Next complete Exam 4 by answering questions 11-20 on pages 8/11-13. (You should have already answered questions 1-10 as part of your study of lesson 7.)

SELF CHECK TEST 8

HOW MUCH HAVE YOU LEARNED?

In the right-hand margin circle the following statements "True" or "False":

1. Nahum prophesied sometime between the fall of Israel and the destruction of Assyria (p. 8/1). (T) F

2. Like Jonah before him, Nahum warned the Assyrians that if they did not repent they would be destroyed utterly (p. 8/1). T (F)

3. One of the great problems which perplexed Habakkuk was why God would punish sinful Judah at the hands of the even more sinful Babylonians (pp. 8/1, 2). (T) F

4. God told Habakkuk that those who trusted in the Lord would be saved; all others would be destroyed (p. 8/2). (T) F

5. Habakkuk was far from satisfied with the answer God gave to him when he wrestled with the moral problem of sin and its punishment (p. 8/2). (T) F

6. The two main themes of Zephaniah's prophecy are God's judgment and God's joy (p. 8/2). (T) F

7. Both Haggai and Zechariah urged the returned remnant of the Jews to rebuild their Temple (p. 8/2). (T) F

8. Zechariah foretold the Lord's triumphal entry into Jerusalem and His subsequent betrayal (p. 8/3). (T) F

9. Malachi prophesied about five hundred years before Christ (p. 8/4). T (F)

10. The people of Malachi's day at once acknowledged their sinful condition when God pointed it out to them through the ministry of His prophet (p. 8/4). T (F)

Turn to the end of the book for the answers to these questions. Do NOT send them to the Correspondence School.

SUMMARY OF THE BIBLE

Exam 4
Lessons 7, 8

Name_____Elsie Mathew_____
(print plainly)

Exam
Grade_____

Address_____

City_____State_____ Zip Code_____ Class Number_____

Instructor_____

LESSON 7

In the blank space in the right-hand margin write the letter of the correct answer.

1. The background of Hosea's prophecy was
   a. trouble and tragedy in Hosea's relationship with his wife
   b. the death of Hosea's mother, the circumstances of which furnished Hosea with analogies with which to illustrate the moral sickness of Israel
   c. rising anger in the nation over inflation and related economic woes, all of which Hosea said were but portents of impending doom.
   d. an outbreak of war between the rival nations of Israel and Judah

_A_

2. The prophecy of Hosea brings to the fore and especially emphasizes
   a. the wrath and anger of God
   b. the tender, patient love of God
   c. the wisdom and omniscience of God
   d. the power of God as Creator and Sustainer of the universe

_B_

8/7

3. Joel's predictions centered around
    a. a plague of locusts
    b. a potential foreign invasion
    c. the coming "Day of the Lord"
    d. the outpouring of God's Spirit on the day of Pentecost
    e. the outpouring of God's Spirit at the end of the age when Israel is restored
    f. all the above
    g. just the first three of the above
    h. none of the above

    F

4. Edom was denounced by
    a. Joel and Amos
    b. Obadiah and Amos
    c. Jonah and Obadiah
    d. Micah and Amos
    e. Obadiah, Micah and Amos

     B

5. Amos was
    a. the prophet of that love "which many waters cannot quench"
    b. a popular prophet so long as he denounced the Gentiles
    c. "the Jeremiah of the northern kingdom," a broken hearted prophet who wept out his predictions of doom against Israel
    d. the only minor prophet who preached to the northern kingdom of Israel

    D

6. Micah prophesied of the Lord Jesus that He would be
    a. born in Bethlehem
    b. raised in Nazareth
    c. preceded by John the Baptist
    d. baptized in Jordan
    e. crucified in Jerusalem

     A

Study the following chart and then answer questions 7-10. You may review lesson 6 before completing these questions and you may review the chart on page 6/2. Note: This chart is not drawn to accurate scale.

	KINGS OF JUDAH	KINGS OF ISRAEL	
Micah	Jehoash	Jehoahaz	Joel
		Jehoash	
	Amaziah	Uzziah	Jonah
	Jeroboam II		Amos
		Zechariah	
		Shallum	
	Jotham	Menahem	Hosea
		Pekahiah	
Isaiah	Ahaz	Pekah	
Jeremiah	Hezekiah	Hoshea	
	Manasseh.		
	Amon		
	Josiah		
	Jehoahaz		
	Jehoiakim		
	Jehoiachin		
	Zedekiah		

Obadiah

Ezekiel
Daniel

7. On the above chart the kings wrongly placed are
   a. Ahaz and Hezekiah; Ahaz was the son of Hezekiah and therefore follows rather than precedes him
   b. Zedekiah and Hoshea; Zedekiah was the last king of Israel and Hoshea was the last king of Judah
   c. Uzziah and Jeroboam II; Uzziah was a king of Judah and Jeroboam II was a king of Israel
   d. the first five kings of Israel who should appear in the inverse order to that listed

8. On the chart Micah is wrongly placed. He belongs
   a. prior to the reign of Jehoash
   b. in the days of Uzziah
   c. in the reigns of Jotham, Ahaz and Hezekiah
   d. in the captivity period with Ezekiel and Daniel

9. On this chart Jeremiah
   a. is rightly placed as coming right after Isaiah
   b. was really a prophet to the northern kingdom and belongs
      on the opposite side of the chart in the reigns of the last
      three kings of Israel
   c. belongs towards the end of the reign of Uzziah; he was the
      "morning star" of the major prophets
   d. belongs at the closing period of the kingdom of Judah

10. On this chart Obadiah is placed
    a. correctly for all are agreed that he ministered at the end of
       the Judean kingdom
    b. incorrectly for all are agreed that he was the earliest of the
       writing prophets
    c. correctly if the assumption is true that he ministered at the
       end of the Judean kingdom; however some believe that he
       belongs at a much earlier period
    d. incorrectly for he was a post-exilic prophet and should ap-
       pear on the chart much further down in the history of the
       nation

WHAT DO YOU SAY?

Read the book of Jonah. What is one lesson from this book that you can apply
to your life?

Obey the Lord; otherwise He will chastise you untill God's plan is fulfilled in you. God is a God of mercy and Love. He forgive our sins if we repent.

LESSON 8

In the blank space in the right-hand margin write the letter of the correct answer.

11. Nahum foretold the complete overthrow of
    a. Jerusalem
    b. Samaria
    c. Babylon
    d. Nineveh

12. The overthrow predicted by Nahum was looked upon by him as
    a. a tragedy for his own countrymen
    b. an occasion for great rejoicing in Judah and one which should be celebrated with a national holiday
    c. just retribution on a people whose wickedness called for judgment
    d. something without moral justification and which posed a real ethical problem which greatly disturbed him

13. Habakkuk's prophecy grappled with
    a. the mystery of God's Person
    b. the problem of pain
    c. the question of sin and its punishment
    d. the problem of election and predestination
    e. inherent problems in the overthrow of Nineveh by the Babylonians

14. The great precept: "The just shall live by faith" occurs three times in the New Testament. It was first given by God to
    a. Nahum
    b. Habakkuk
    c. Zephaniah
    d. Haggai

15. Zephaniah traces Judah's doom to its
    a. vacillating foreign policy
    b. neglect of the Lord's day
    c. idolatrous worship
    d. disloyal troops
    e. alliance with Egypt

16. Which of the following was NOT included in Zephaniah's prophecies?
   a. Ammon
   b. Assyria
   c. Babylon
   d. Ethiopia
   e. Moab
   f. Philistia

_c_

17. Haggai's prophecy was almost entirely concerned with
   a. the Lord's first coming
   b. the Lord's second coming
   c. the rebuilding of the Jerusalem Temple
   d. idolatry and its evils
   e. the wickedness of the Gentile neighbors of Judah

_c_

18. Zechariah's eight visions are
   a. highly symbolic in form
   b. restricted in scope to the time period in which the prophet lived
   c. concerned solely with the Gentile nations
   d. what comprise his entire prophecy

_A_

19. Which minor prophet tells us more than any of the others about the Lord Jesus?
   a. Nahum
   b. Habakkuk
   c. Zephaniah
   d. Haggai
   e. Isaiah
   f. Zechariah
   g. Malachi
   h. Micah

_F_

20. The Day of the Lord is a theme of
   a. Nahum, Habakkuk and Zephaniah
   b. Obadiah and Haggai
   c. Joel, Zephaniah and Malachi
   d. Zephaniah, Zechariah and Haggai

_c_

WHAT DO YOU SAY?

The five abuses of Malachi's day are prevalent in the Church today. Which one convicts you most personally and what are you doing about it?

People display a lack of Love for the Lord.
Love of money and materialism increasing day
by day. I am praying for the believers. Also
I am very careful for myself. Let our Good Lord
open our Eyes to see the situation and turn to the
Lord.

Lesson 9

Christ and His Church

THE GOSPELS

The Gospels are the heart of the Bible because they reveal the central Person of all time, the Lord Jesus Christ. History is indeed His story, and in the Gospels we find His story written by the hand of God.

The life of the Savior on earth covered a span of about 33 years. We read first of His virgin birth in a manger at Bethlehem, of His parents' flight into Egypt, and then of their return to Nazareth. When He was twelve, we find Him at the Passover Feast in Jerusalem, but from that time until He was thirty, the story of His life is shrouded in silence.

At thirty, the Lord was baptized by John the Baptist, then tempted by Satan in the wilderness for forty days. Immediately after this, He entered upon what is known as His public ministry—a ministry that, for convenience, can be divided into three parts: (1) in Judea—about one year; (2) In Galilee—about one year and nine months; (3) In Perea—about four or five months.

His ministry was characterized by certain features: (1) He performed many miracles in order to vindicate His claim to be the Son of God and the King of Israel. (2) He taught the people great truths concerning the Kingdom of God—how it is entered, and how its subjects are expected to behave. In doing so, He used parables, illustrations and Old Testament quotations. (3) He called, trained and sent forth twelve disciples to proclaim the Gospel to the Jews.

As His message met increasing opposition and hatred from His own people, He widened His ministry to the Gentiles, proclaiming Himself to be the Savior of all who would receive Him by faith. Several times He predicted His own death and resurrection, and prophesied terrible suffering for the nation of Israel that was about to reject Him.

At the end of His Perean ministry, He made His triumphal entry into Jerusalem, and was wildly acclaimed by the people. However, the religious leaders were plotting against Him, and bargained with Judas to betray Him.

When the Lord Jesus returned to Jerusalem, it was to keep the Passover with His disciples, and also to institute the Lord's Supper as a lasting remembrance of Him in His death. Then followed in quick succession His agony in the Garden of Gethsemane, His betrayal, the Jewish trial (at which Peter vigorously denied his Lord), and the Roman trials before both Pilate and Herod.

Although the Son of God was obviously innocent, having been accused only by false witnesses, yet Pilate bowed to the desires of the people and delivered Him to be crucified. Hanging on a cross between two thieves, the Savior died in agony and blood. In one sense, He was killed by the hands of wicked men. But in another sense, He went to the cross willingly in order to bear God's judgment on sin, so that sinners believing on Him might be saved.

His body was buried in the new tomb of Joseph of Arimathea, and on the third day, He rose from among the dead. Thereafter, He made frequent appearances to His disciples and to other believers until forty days later when He ascended up into heaven to be exalted at the right hand of God the Father—a Prince and a Savior.

Not all the things that Jesus did are written in the Gospels. In fact, if His complete life story were written, the world itself could not contain the books (John 21:25). "But these are written that ye might believe that Jesus is the Christ, the Son of God; and that believing ye might have life through His Name" (John 20:31).

The Gospels are unique in all literature in that they present four separate accounts of a perfect, sinless Man. The Lord's life is so real and natural that we feel He is one of us; yet His life is so perfect that no one can find a blemish in it. No mere man could write the life story of a sinless person. In the Gospels, the Holy Spirit has given us *four* such records.

But why are there four Gospels? Would not one have been enough? The answer simply is that the four writers present the Lord Jesus Christ in a different manner, or with a different purpose.

MATTHEW introduces the Lord Jesus as the Son of David and King of the Jews. We see the Messiah in His birth, then announced by John the Baptist, tested, manifested and rejected. Because Matthew's first concern is in presenting Christ as King of the Jews, he traces His genealogy back to David and Abraham.

MARK describes the Son of God as a Servant—the One who came into the world to do His Father's will. No genealogy is given inasmuch as the servant's work is of greater importance than his ancestry.

LUKE's object is to present the Lord Jesus as Son of Man. Thus the genealogy in chapter 3 goes back to Adam, the first man. In Luke's Gospel, we see the Lord as a Man among men, serving, seeking and saving them.

JOHN's Gospel is very different from the others. Here Christ is set forth as the Son of God. No genealogy is given; instead, He is described as the Word who was in the beginning, the eternal God. Another important difference is that John alone describes the Judean ministry of the Savior; the other writers deal with His Galilean and Perean ministries.

Because we have these four distinct accounts of the Lord, it is possible for us to know Him in a more complete and more intimate way than His disciples knew Him when He was on earth. For this, we should be deeply and everlastingly grateful.

THE ACTS OF THE APOSTLES

This book is a brief history of the formation and early growth of the Christian church. Some have called it the Acts of the Holy Spirit because He is the guiding Person throughout. In a sense, it is also the Acts of two apostles—Peter and Paul.

Peter's ministry is prominent in the first twelve chapters. It begins on the Day of Pentecost when the Holy Spirit descended and the church was born. Peter's preaching emphasized the resurrection and the

Paul's First Missionary Journey

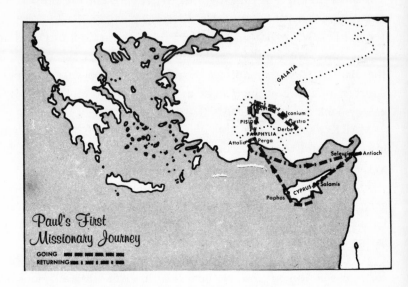

Paul's Second Missionary Journey

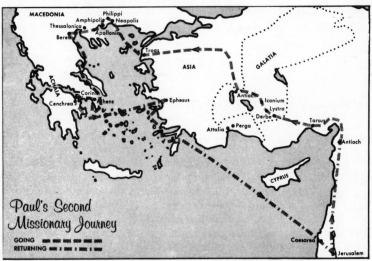

Paul's Third Missionary Journey

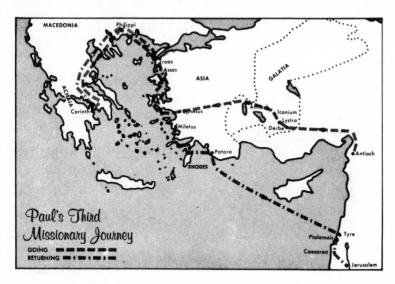

The Journey to Rome

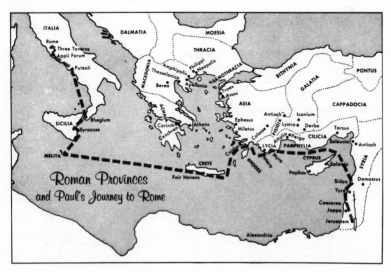

Lordship of Christ. The church thus begun at Jerusalem was almost entirely made up of Jewish converts.

Then persecution set in and increased in intensity until finally Stephen was arrested and stoned to death—the first martyr of the church. Now the believers scattered throughout Judea and Samaria, preaching the Gospel wherever they went. Against his own personal desires, Peter was instructed to carry the good news to Gentiles also, and from this point the church was no longer limited to Jews. In fact, as the Jewish nation continued to reject the message, the church's membership became increasingly Gentile.

From Acts 13:4 to the end of the book, the principal person is Paul. Saved while on the way to persecute Christians in Damascus, Paul undertook his mission as apostle to the Gentiles, just as Peter had served as apostle to the Jews. His ministry may be divided into three main missionary journeys (see maps), and then a trip to Rome as a prisoner.

First Missionary Journey—Beginning at Antioch in Syria, Paul carried the message of Christ to Cyprus and several cities in Asia Minor.

Second Missionary Journey—Again Paul visited Asia Minor, then sailed across to Macedonia and Greece, finally returning to Antioch via Ephesus and Caesarea. It was during these travels that he wrote his two letters to the THESSALONIANS.

Third Missionary Journey—This trip took Paul through Asia Minor, Macedonia, Greece, then back along the western and southern coasts of Asia Minor to Jerusalem. While on this tour, he wrote I and II CORINTHIANS, ROMANS and GALATIANS.

On his way home from his third tour, Paul was repeatedly warned not to go to Jerusalem because of the danger of arrest, imprisonment and possibly death. He persisted in going, however, and shortly after his arrival was falsely accused by some Asiatic Jews of profaning the temple. He was tried before the Sanhedrin, then before Felix, Festus and Agrippa, but since he appealed to the Emperor, he was sent to Rome for trial before Caesar. The ship was wrecked at Melita so crew and passengers had to winter there. When Paul finally reached Rome, he was allowed the liberty of his own hired house. There he spent two years, ministering the Word of God to all whom he could contact, and writing his prison epistles—EPHESIANS, PHILIPPIANS, COLOSSIANS and PHILEMON.

Although the Book of Acts ends at this point in the history, there is considerable evidence that Paul won his freedom after this first imprisonment and that he travelled extensively again. It was during this time, no doubt, that he wrote I TIMOTHY, TITUS and also HEBREWS (if Paul was the author of this letter).

It is believed that Paul was then taken to Rome a second time and imprisoned. His second letter to TIMOTHY doubtless was penned at this time, shortly before his execution.

When you have mastered this lesson, take the Self-Check Test on page 9/9. Look up the answers to this test and see how well you did.

Then take the first part of Exam 5 (covering lesson 9), questions 1-10 on pages 10/7-9 (right after lesson 10).

SELF CHECK TEST 9

ARE YOU MAKING PROGRESS?

In the right-hand margin circle the following statements "True" or "False":

1. The Lord Jesus lived on earth for about thirty-three years altogether (p. 9/1). (T) F

2. The Lord's public ministry was in Judea, Galilee and Perea (p. 9/1). (T) F

3. The miracles Jesus performed proved Him to be the Son of God and the Messiah of Israel (p. 9/1). (T) F

4. The Lord Jesus had to face three trials, one before the Jews and two before the Gentiles before He was finally condemned to death (p. 9/2). (T) F

5. The only way to look at Christ's death on the cross is as a gross travesty of justice (p. 9/2). (T) F

6. The Gospels contain a complete record of all that the Lord Jesus said and did throughout the period of His public ministry (p. 9/2). (T) F

7. The four writers of the Gospels all present the story of Jesus from the identical viewpoint (p. 9/3). T (F)

8. The Church was born on the Day of Pentecost (p. 9/3). (T) F

9. God raised up Paul to be the apostle to the Gentiles just as He commissioned Peter to be the apostle to the Jews (p. 9/7). (T) F

10. During his first imprisonment at Rome, the apostle Paul wrote four of the books of the New Testament (pp. 9/7, 8). T (F)

Turn to the end of the book for the answers to these questions. Do NOT send them to the Correspondence School.

9/8

From the Pen of Paul

ROMANS

Just as the Acts gives the history of the church, so the epistles present the great teachings or doctrines of the church. Romans, for instance, sets forth the doctrine of justification by faith. (Justification means that God looks upon a sinner as fit for heaven the moment that sinner puts his faith in the Lord Jesus Christ.) In this letter, Paul first shows that all men are sinners and therefore guilty before God. He then tells how the Lord Jesus Christ died as a substitute for sinners, so that men can be saved simply by believing on Him. In this connection, he emphasizes that (1) salvation is by faith and not by keeping the law or by good works; (2) Gentiles as well as Jews can be saved in this way; (3) no one was ever saved in any other way, even in Old Testament times.

After describing the wonderful benefits of justification, Paul emphasizes that this free salvation encourages holy living. Christians consider themselves as having died and having been buried with Christ. Now they live with the object of pleasing God. The indwelling Holy Spirit gives them the power to live in a godly manner.

To the objection that the Gospel disregards God's past promises to the nation of Israel, Paul shows that Israel's present condition of being set aside is neither complete nor final. God will fulfill His promises when a believing portion of the nation receives the Lord Jesus as its Messiah.

The last five chapters are filled with practical instructions as to how justified persons should behave in their dealings with God, with civil government, with the world, and with their fellow-believers.

By many, the Epistle to the Romans is considered to be the most important single presentation of fundamental Christian doctrine.

I CORINTHIANS

Paul's first letter to the church in Corinth arose from reports he heard about troubles there, and also from questions which he had been asked by some of the believers. It will be seen from the following list of subjects dealt with that the conduct of the church's affairs is in view:

1. Divisions and strife in the church (chs. 1—4). The Corinthians were exalting human leaders, and had to be rebuked for such carnality.
2. Sin committed by one of the members (ch. 5). The church should not countenance this, but should exclude the brother until he confessed and forsook his sin.
3. Christians going to law against each other (ch. 6:1-11). This is forbidden; they should be able to settle such matters among themselves.
4. Personal impurity (ch. 6). This, too, is condemned; the Christian's body is the temple of the Holy Spirit.
5. Marriage (ch. 7). Paul teaches that marriage is not compulsory, that sometimes it is expedient to remain single. However, the general rule is that men and women should marry, in view of prevailing immorality.
6. Meats sacrificed to idols (chs. 8—10). While it is not wrong to eat such meat, we should not do anything that would offend another Christian.
7. Women's place in public worship (ch. 11:1-16). Women should wear a covering on their head as a testimony to the angels of their subjection.
8. The Lord's Supper (ch. 11:17-34). This feast should only be eaten after searching self-examination.
9. Spiritual gifts (chs. 12—14). The most spectacular gifts are not always the best. Indeed, they are all worthless without love.

10. The Resurrection (ch. 15). Chapter 15 is one of the outstanding passages on the doctrine of the resurrection of the body.
11. The care of the poor (ch. 16). The epistle closes with instructions for systematic giving on the part of the church to the poor.

II CORINTHIANS

There are two main themes in this letter. The first and most prominent is the apostle's defense of his own ministry. Apparently some enemies of the truth had arisen in Corinth, denying that Paul was a true apostle of the Lord Jesus. In reply to these charges, Paul here describes the greatness of the ministry which had been committed to him, and how severely he had suffered in carrying out his appointed task. He compares his service with that of these false teachers, and reminds the Corinthians that they themselves were proof of the genuineness of his work, i.e., they had been saved through him.

Then a second subject is a moving appeal by Paul to send financial help to the suffering and needy saints in Jerusalem. The Corinthians should imitate the generosity of the Lord Jesus, who though He was rich, yet became poor, that we through His poverty might be rich.

GALATIANS

After Paul had visited Galatia and founded churches there, false teachers began to deny his authority as an apostle and to teach the Christians that circumcision and obedience to the law were necessary for salvation. In this letter, Paul first of all shows that his authority was from the Lord Jesus alone and that therefore his message was divine. He then insists that salvation is entirely by grace and not by law-keeping. The law can only curse and condemn those who fail to keep it; it cannot give life. God gave the law to show men their need of a Savior. Once they are saved, they are redeemed from the curse of the law; henceforth Christ and not the law is their rule of life. Then Paul closes by encouraging the saints to live in the enjoyment of Christian liberty and not to allow themselves to be put under the bondage of the law. He reminds them that the cross spells the end of their personal efforts to obtain salvation, and that now they live by the power of the Holy Spirit, not by the energy of the flesh.

When you are ready, take Self-Check Test 10 and then grade your answers.

Next complete Exam 5 by answering questions 11-20 on pages 10/10-12. (You should have already answered questions 1-10 as part of your study of lesson 9.)

SELF CHECK TEST 10

HOW MUCH DO YOU REMEMBER?

In the right-hand margin circle the following statements "True" or "False":

1. The epistles record the great doctrines and teachings of the Church (p. 10/1). **(T)   F**

2. The great theme of Romans is Church government (p. 10/1). **T   (F)**

3. According to the book of Romans men are saved by faith in the Lord Jesus alone (p. 10/1). **(T)   F**

4. Romans teaches that when a person is saved he must live accordingly—he must have a belief that behaves (p. 10/1). **(T)   F**

5. In writing to the Romans, Paul conspicuously ignores any reference to the Jews (p. 10/1). **T   (F)**

6. I Corinthians begins by dealing with discords and divisions in the Church at Corinth (p. 10/2). **(T)   F**

7. Paul taught the Corinthians that it was consistent with a good Christian testimony to sue a brother in a secular court if the circumstances warranted (p. 10/2). **T   (F)**

8. Paul taught the Corinthians to seek the most spectacular gifts because these were the most important ones (p. 10/2). **T   (F)**

9. Paul made it a point never to mention money matters when writing to Christians (p. 10/3). **T   (F)**

10. The basic issue dealt with in Paul's letter to the Galatians is that of legalism—thinking that a set of rules and regulations (such as the Law of Moses) is a basic part of Christianity (p. 10/3). **T   (F)**

Turn to the end of the book for the answers to these questions. Do NOT send them to the Correspondence School.

SUMMARY OF THE BIBLE

Exam 5
Lessons 9, 10

Name _Elsie Mathew_
(print plainly)

Exam
Grade_____

Address_____

City_____ State_____ Zip Code_____ Class Number_____

Instructor_____

LESSON 9

In the blank space in the right-hand margin write the letter of the correct answer.

1. The Lord Jesus spent the years of His public ministry
   a. mostly in Judea
   b. mostly in Galilee
   c. mostly in Perea
   d. equally in all three places
   e. equally so far as Judea and Galilee were concerned but with an additional four or five months in Perea

2. Which of the following did the Lord Jesus NOT do when He was on earth? He
   a. performed miracles to prove His Deity and Messiahship
   b. called and trained twelve disciples
   c. revealed vital truths concerning the kingdom of God
   d. preached in various Gentile cities outside the limits of Palestine
   e. foretold His own death, burial and resurrection
   f. prophesied that the Jewish nation would suffer for its rejection of Him

3. Pilate ordered Christ's crucifixion because
   a. he believed Him to be guilty of the charges brought against Him by the Jews
   b. he sympathized with the Jewish cause and, like the Jewish leaders, believed Jesus to be a blasphemer
   c. he wanted to placate the Jewish people
   d. he was deceived by the false witnesses the Jews brought into court to testify against Jesus

4. The four Gospels contain
  a. a complete record of all that Jesus said and did
  b. enough of the story of Jesus to bring people to a saving faith in Him
  c. much about Jesus but leave serious gaps in the story leaving us without vital facts we need
  d. the story of a sinless life conceived by sinful men _B_

5. Matthew's account of the Lord Jesus emphasizes Jesus as the
  a. Son of Man
  b. Son of God
  c. King of the Jews
  d. Servant of Jehovah _C_

6. Which of the following best states the case?
  a. Matthew's genealogy of the Lord Jesus traces His ancestry without break back to Adam, the first man
  b. Mark's account of the Lord Jesus emphasizes the Servant character of the Lord and therefore is best suited to his purpose in writing
  c. Luke is satisfied with tracing the Lord's ancestry back to David and leaving it there because Matthew had already traced it back to Adam
  d. John emphasizes the eternal Godhead of Jesus so ignores His human ancestry _B_

7. The most prominent persons in the book of Acts are
  a. Peter, James and John
  b. Peter and Paul
  c. Stephen and Simon Peter
  d. Paul and Barnabas _B_

8. Peter's greatest ministry in the book of Acts was to
  a. the Jews although he did also open the door of the Church to the Gentiles
  b. the Gentiles although he did first open the door of the Church to the Jews
  c. the Samaritans although at first he was reluctant to go to the despised city of Samaria
  d. Rome where he preached to both Jew and Gentile _A_

9. On which of his three missionary journeys, recorded in the book of Acts, did Paul write to the Corinthians and to the Romans?

a. his first missionary journey
b. his second missionary journey
c. his third missionary journey
d. he wrote to them from prison in Caesarea

_c_

10. Paul's great ambition was to preach the Gospel in Rome. When he finally arrived at Rome

a. it was to found the first Christian Church ever to be established in the capital of the Roman Empire
b. it was to found the first Christian Church in the continent of Europe
c. it was as a prisoner to appear for trial before Caesar
d. it was at the beginning of his third missionary journey
e. it was as the honored guest of the Emperor who was anxious to hear the gospel from the lips of the great apostle to the Gentiles

_c_

WHAT DO YOU SAY?

What is your personal relationship to the Lord Jesus Christ?

Lord Jesus christ is the Lord of my life. He is my master and my best friend, helper and comfort and companion at all time. I talk to him, walk with Him and waiting to see Him face to face - Soon - Till then I will Serve Him.

LESSON 10

In the blank space in the right-hand margin write the letter of the correct answer.

11. The great theme of Romans is
a. the second coming of Christ
b. conduct in the Church
c. justification by faith
d. the wealth, walk and warfare of the Christian life

12. Paul's letter to the Romans begins
a. by explaining exactly how people can be saved
b. by showing men why they need to be saved
c. with an explanation of the special place of privilege the Jew occupies in the plan of God for this age
d. a warning to backsliders

13. According to the book of Romans
a. salvation results in holy living
b. salvation depends on whether or not we have earned it
c. salvation for the Jew is by works and for the Gentile by faith
d. salvation is in the future tense only thus a person can only know whether or not he is saved after he dies

14. In Romans 9-11 Paul discusses the relationship of the Gospel to the nation of Israel. He concludes that
a. because of the rejection of the Messiah, God has set aside the Jewish nation and cancelled all its special privileges and promises
b. God's grace has so overruled this nation's rejection of the Messiah that it is just as though Calvary never happened so far as the Jew is concerned; thus he still enjoys all that was given and promised in the Old Testament
c. at the present time the Jewish nation has been set aside but eventually it will be restored to its former place and privilege when the remnant of the nation accepts Jesus as Messiah
d. God foresaw the Jewish rejection of Christ and deemed it necessary in order to bring about the crucifixion without which salvation would be impossible for men; therefore the Jews are not to blame for what they did to Jesus

15. The last five chapters of Romans contain mostly
   a. doctrinal matters
   b. prophetic truths
   c. historical allusions
   d. practical instructions
   e. biographical details

_D_

16. I Corinthians was written by Paul to
   a. advise the Church there that he was sending Timothy to them to investigate their disorders
   b. deal with problems which had arisen
   c. ask the Corinthian Christians to be more generous in supporting the Lord's work
   d. thoroughly explain the principles of theology relating to salvation

_B_

17. One of the members of the Corinthian Church had committed a particularly flagrant form of sin. Paul advised the Church to
   a. excommunicate this brother
   b. greatly question the reality of this man's salvation
   c. be tolerant of the sin because anyone could fall into sin
   d. urge the man to come back to Church in the hope that he would repent under the preaching of the Word

_A_

18. Which of the following best summarizes the teaching of I Corinthians? It deals primarily with
   a. prophecy
   b. church truth
   c. the doctrine of inspiration
   d. foreign missions

_B_

19. II Corinthians was written by Paul to refute the false teachers at Corinth who claimed that
   a. the Day of the Lord had already come
   b. Paul was not really an apostle
   c. salvation is by works not by faith alone
   d. water baptism is essential to salvation
   e. the Lord Jesus was truly God but that His humanity was unreal
   f. the Lord Jesus was truly Man but that He was not truly God
   g. marriage rendered a person unfit for the Christian ministry

_B_

20. In Galatians Paul shows that
   a. a person can be saved by doing his best to keep God's law
   b. we are saved by faith alone but kept by keeping the law of Moses
   c. the law of God is an instrument of accusation and condemnation rather than of salvation
   d. the only law which applies to the believer today is the law to keep the Sabbath day

_____ c

WHAT DO YOU SAY?

State one truth from I Corinthians which has been especially helpful to you.

our body is the temple of God. Personal impurity will defile the body of christ. Since the Holy spirit dwell in us we need to be cautious and say 'NO' to any sins.

Lesson 11

More Letters from Paul

EPHESIANS

The first three chapters of this letter describe the wonderful position into which God has brought all true believers; they are "in Christ," that is, they enjoy the same favor and acceptance before God as the Lord Jesus does. Instead of being blessed with material riches on the earth, the child of God is blessed with every spiritual blessing in the heavenlies in Christ. These blessings include redemption, forgiveness of sins, acceptance in Christ, adoption and the gift of the Holy Spirit. In chapters two and three, Paul unfolds the truth that all believers, Jew and Gentile, are members of the church, and that Christ is the chief cornerstone. This church will be an eternal display of the wisdom of God to the heavenly hosts.

The last three chapters tell the believers to walk worthily of their great privileges. They are to live in peace with one another; to employ the gifts which Christ gave for the building up of the church; and in general to be followers of God.

PHILIPPIANS

Like Ephesians, this epistle was written while Paul was a prisoner in Rome. However, as someone has said, it does not have "the slightest smell of a prison" about it. Instead, Paul found a great deal for which to rejoice, showing that a Christian's joy is based on Christ and not on earthly circumstances. Paul expresses deep thanks for the money which the Philippians had sent to him by faithful Epaphroditus. He rejoices that his imprisonment has resulted in the spread of the Gospel, and, even if he is condemned, "to die is gain." He encourages the saints to fulfill his joy by unity and humility, after the example of Christ; warns them against false teachers; and shows them how, in running the Christian race, he counts all earthly honors and attainments as loss for Christ. In closing, the great apostle stresses the need for unity, rejoicing, self-control, prayerful trust, and pure thought-life; once again he thanks them for their gifts to him and assures them that God will supply all their needs according to His riches in glory by Christ Jesus.

COLOSSIANS

It appears that the saints in Colosse were in danger of becoming occupied with philosophy, traditions, ordinances and law-keeping. In writing this letter to them, Paul seeks rather to occupy them with the glories of the Lord Jesus Christ. He emphasizes that Christ is the Creator and Sustainer, the very image of God, and the Head of the body—the church. They should realize the pre-eminence of His Person and the all-sufficiency of His work. Since they are complete in Him, they should not wander off into human religions, but should set their affections on the risen Christ, and live as those who are risen with Him. Practical instructions on how to do this are given at the close.

I THESSALONIANS

This is believed to be the first letter written by Paul. In every chapter, he introduces the return of the Lord Jesus Christ, though with a different purpose in each.

Chapter 1—Christ's coming is the blessed hope of all those who are converted.

Chapter 2—The Lord's return will mean joy and reward for all faithful service done for Him.

Chapter 3—Christians should love one another and live holy lives in view of His advent.

Chapter 4—It is a comfort to know that saints who have died will be raised at His coming; living saints will rise with them to meet Him and to be forever with Him.

Chapter 5—Christ's return will begin the day of the Lord as far as the unbelieving world is concerned. This "day" will be a time of tribulation and wrath. In view of these imminent events, Christians should live soberly and expectantly.

II THESSALONIANS

In his first letter, Paul mentioned the day of the Lord as a time of great suffering. Because of the intense persecutions they were enduring, some of the Thessalonians began to worry that they were in it. The apostle writes this letter to show that this was impossible: (1) Christ will come for His saints first and they will be gathered together unto Him; (2) Then there will be a great departure from the faith, or apostasy; (3) The man of sin, also known as the Antichrist, will be revealed.

The prospect of Christ's return should be a comfort to all true believers. Christians should not cease working while they await His return. Rather, they should earn their living quietly and never grow weary in well-doing.

I TIMOTHY

This first letter to Timothy is primarily concerned with order in the church. Chapter one, for instance, stresses the importance of maintaining sound doctrine. Chapter two deals with the matter of prayer and also instructs women to dress modestly and to refrain from public ministry in the church. The qualifications of elders and deacons are given in detail in chapter three. Then, in the last three chapters, Paul instructs Timothy concerning the exercise of his ministry; concerning the treatment of elders and widows; and concerning the duties of servants. He exhorts him to be faithful in guarding the trust which was committed to him, and commends him to the grace of God.

II TIMOTHY

This letter was written from Rome, during Paul's last imprisonment. As the apostle looked about him, he saw departure from the truth and increasing difficulties for the church. In view of these conditions, he exhorts young Timothy to be brave and unashamed in the discharge of his responsibilities. As the darkness around him deepens, Timothy should train others as teachers, endure hardness as a good soldier, and stay away from evil of every kind. Paul predicts that the last days will be characterized by terrible wickedness in life and doctrine; Timothy's great resource is the Word of God. Finally, the apostle charges Timothy solemnly to carry on his work faithfully, preaching the Word, watching, enduring—in short, making full proof of his ministry.

TITUS

Between his two Roman imprisonments, Paul had left Titus in Crete to see that order was established and maintained in the churches there. The Epistle to Titus lists some of the necessities for an orderly church. First of all, the bishops or elders must meet certain important qualifications. Secondly, evil teachers must be stopped. Thirdly, sound doctrine must be taught and obeyed. Finally, the saints should be subject to worldly powers and should devote themselves to good works rather than to idle speculations.

PHILEMON

There are three principal characters in this book: Philemon, Onesimus and Paul. Philemon was a Christian who lived in Colosse and was a close friend of Paul. Onesimus was his slave who ran away from him, went to Rome where he met Paul in prison, and was saved through the apostle. In this letter, Paul asks Philemon to receive Onesimus back, not now as a slave, but as a brother in the Lord. Paul offers to pay any loss incurred by Onesimus, by telling Philemon, "Put that on mine account." This, of course, is a lovely picture of the Gospel, showing how Christ took our sins and charged them to His account.

When you have mastered this lesson, take the Self-Check Test on page 11/6. Look up the answers to this test and see how well you did.

Then take the first part of Exam 6 (covering lesson 11), questions 1-10 on pages 12/7-9 (right after lesson 12).

WHAT HAVE YOU LEARNED?

In the right-hand margin circle the following statements "True" or "False":

1. The blessings God has for His people today are spiritual rather than material (p. 11/1). (T)   F

2. In Ephesians, Paul tells the Christians that they should employ their gifts and talents to build up their family fortunes (p. 11/1). T   (F)

3. One of the reasons for Paul's writing to the Philippians was to express thanks for a gift of money (p. 11/2). (T)   F

4. The dominating theme of Colossians is the Person and pre-eminence of the Lord Jesus Christ (p. 11/2). (T)   F

5. The theme of the Lord's coming runs through I Thessalonians and in each chapter Paul reintroduces the theme from the same point of view and for the same purpose (p. 11/2). X(T)   F

6. A mistaken concept of the "Day of the Lord" on the part of the Thessalonians prompted Paul to write them his second epistle (p. 11/3). (T)   F

7. Paul discusses the qualifications of elders and deacons in his first letter to Timothy (p. 11/3). (T)   F

8. By the time of Paul's second Roman imprisonment, heresy had taken deep root in the Church. Paul's second letter to Timothy is therefore remarkably free from any reference to apostasy (p. 11/4). X(T)   F

9. Titus and I Timothy have much in common (p. 11/4). X(T)   F

10. The letter to Philemon remarkably illustrates the Gospel (p. 11/5): (T)   F

Turn to the end of the book for the answers to these questions. Do NOT send them to the Correspondence School.

Lesson 12

Look Out! Look Up!

HEBREWS

The author of this letter is unknown. Many presume it to be one of Paul's letters, and that is why it is included in this section. However, the safest position is to say that we do not know definitely.

The purpose of the letter is clear. Many of the first inquirers into the Christian faith were Jews. They heard the Gospel preached and became interested. Some even professed faith in Christ. However, the simplicity of Christianity was in marked contrast to the colorful ceremonies of Judaism. Thus, many of them were tempted to turn away from Christ, Whom they could not see, to a temple, an altar, a priesthood and sacrifices which they could see. The writer of this letter to the Hebrews, therefore, shows the superiority of Christianity to all that ever went before it. Instead of worshipping in a man-made tabernacle, for instance, we enter by faith into the presence of God in heaven and worship there. Instead of having a priest who is a sinner and who will someday die, we have a Great High Priest who is holy, harmless, undefiled, and who will never die. In other words, the things of Judaism were visible but only temporary and incomplete. They were but the shadows, the types, the pictures of the Person and work of Christ. The things of Christianity, though invisible, are real and eternal. They are seen by faith, and without such faith it is impossible to please God.

JAMES

This letter from James (perhaps a brother of our Lord) to Jewish Christians scattered throughout the then-known world is thought to be the earliest New Testament epistle. It probably was written during the first days of the church when the membership was largely Jewish and when Jewish customs still prevailed.

It is a very practical epistle, rebuking such sins as class distinction, an unbridled tongue, envy, strife and oppression of the poor.

James emphasizes the difference between faith which is mere profession, and that which results in good works. He does not contradict Paul's teaching that we are saved by faith alone, but insists that true faith results in a life of good works.

The epistle closes with exhortations to the saints to be patient in affliction and to pray for one another.

I PETER

Peter's first epistle was written to Christian Jews in modern Asia Minor who were going through intense suffering because of persecution. His message is one of hope. The Christian can look beyond suffering to glory. For the present, God's grace is sufficient for every time of need. As to the future, the wealth of the Christian is incorruptible—the blood of Christ, the Word of God and the future inheritance; persecution can never rob him of these.

Therefore, the apostle urges the saints to stand fast, to look on sufferings as necessary, temporary and helpful, and to suffer for well-doing, not for their own sins. He encourages all to follow Christ's example by holy living and then speaks particularly to them as citizens, slaves, husbands and wives, especially in view of the approaching end of the age. Elders in the church are exhorted to faithfulness, and the younger to obedience and submission.

II PETER

II Peter, like II Thessalonians and II Timothy, speaks of church conditions in the last days, when corruption will be complete in Christendom.

In chapter one, the apostle pleads for the development of Christian character in view of the certainty of the coming kingdom when rewards will be manifest.

Chapter two warns of false teachers who will lead many astray but whose judgment is inescapable.

The last chapter tells of latter-day infidels who will deny the truth of Christ's coming. Peter reaffirms the doctrine of the second advent and the judgment of this world; and exhorts the believers to diligence, holiness, steadfastness and growth in grace in the light of His coming.

I JOHN

In this book, the apostle John describes the traits of those who are members of the family of God. Just as there are striking resemblances in human families, so the children of God are alike in many ways. Some of those likenesses are:

1. They walk in the light rather than in darkness; that is, they no longer have the sin habit.
2. They confess their sins, when they do sin, in order that the happy, family spirit might be maintained.
3. They keep God's commandments.
4. They love the brethren.
5. They confess the Lord Jesus Christ by life and by lip.
6. They possess the Holy Spirit.
7. They overcome the world.

The epistle also corrects false ideas concerning the deity and humanity of the Lord Jesus. He is perfect God and perfect Man. Any other concept of God than is found in Christ is idolatry.

II and III JOHN

It is interesting to contrast these two epistles. II John is a warning against false teachers; the apostle's advice is to keep the door closed to all such.

III John, on the other hand, concerns those who are true believers; the Christians should show hospitality and kindness to them.

Three men are mentioned in III John. Gaius is commended for his godliness and hospitality. Diotrephes is rebuked for his self-importance. Demetrius is praised for his consistent behavior.

JUDE

Jude's epistle has to do with the sin of apostasy, that is, the sin of knowing the truth and abandoning it. He uses three incidents to show how apostasy has been punished: the backsliding Israelites, the fallen angels and the cities of Sodom and Gomorrah. Then he mentions three types of apostasy, illustrated by three Old Testament characters:

Cain—human religion and hatred of God's people.

Balaam—dealing in divine matters for monetary reward.

Core—rebellion against divine rule.

The judgment of all such is certain. Christians should build themselves up in faith, prayer and love, looking for the coming of the Lord.

REVELATION

The apostle John's Revelation of the Lord Jesus Christ looks into the future when all God's purposes for the earth will reach their fulfillment and a new heaven and a new earth will be ushered in. It is helpful to outline the book in the following manner:

Chapters 1–3 contain seven letters to churches in Asia. Though these letters might have been addressed to literal churches in John's day, it is also true that they give an accurate sketch of the church through the various stages of its history, and even predict its condition at the time when the Lord will come again.

Chapters 4 and 5 give us a view of the saints in heaven, gathered around the Throne and worshipping the Lamb. Many believe that this takes place after Christ has returned to take His people home.

Chapters 6—19 describe the terrible judgments which will be poured out on the unbelieving world during the period known as the Tribulation, the time of Jacob's trouble. In describing these judgments, John uses such figurative expressions as the seven seals, the seven trumpets and the seven vials. At the close, the Lord Jesus Christ will personally appear to destroy all His enemies.

Chapters 20—22 tell us that Christ will reign in the earth for 1000 years, during which time Satan will be bound in the bottomless pit. At the end of Christ's earthly reign, He will judge the wicked of all ages and they will be cast into the lake of fire. New heavens and a new earth will follow. God's people, sinless and deathless, will dwell with Him in undisturbed happiness for ever and ever.

It is interesting to notice that while the last book of the Old Testament closes with the word "curse," the final book of the New Testament ends with a blessing.

"The grace of our Lord Jesus Christ be with you all. Amen."

The reason for this is that Calvary comes in between the two.

When you are ready, take Self-Check Test 12 and then grade your answers.

Next complete Exam 6 by answering questions 11-20 on pages 12/10-12. (You should have already answered questions 1-10 as part of your study of lesson 11.)

HOW MUCH HAVE YOU RETAINED?

In the right-hand margin circle the following statements "True" or "False":

1. The author of Hebrews is unquestionably the apostle Paul (p. 12/1).

   T   **(F)**

2. Hebrews shows that the visible things of the Old Testament religion were, in reality, just the shadows which have their substance in the Person and work of Christ (p. 12/1).

   (T)   F

3. James' view of justification by works is at variance with Paul's doctrine of justification by faith (p. 12/2).

   T   **(F)**

4. Peter tells the suffering saints of his day that suffering must be looked upon as a necessity (p. 12/2).

   (T)   F

5. It is only in II Peter that reference is made in the New Testament to the ultimate complete corruption of Christendom (pp. 12/3, 4).

   T   **(F)**

6. One of the traits of being in God's family is that we love God's people (p. 12/3).

   (T)   F

7. In III John Diotrephes is commended and Demetrius is rebuked (p. 12/4)

   T   **(F)**

8. The epistle of Jude centers around the theme of apostasy (p. 12/4).

   (T)   F

9. The letters to the seven churches of Asia were written by various apostles (p. 12/4).

   T   **(F)**

10. Both Old Testament and New Testament end on the very same note (p. 12/5).

    T   **(F)**

Turn to the end of the book for the answers to these questions. Do NOT send them to the Correspondence School.

SUMMARY OF THE BIBLE

Exam 6
Lessons 11, 12

Name _____ Exam Grade _____
(print plainly)

Address _____

City _____ State _____ Zip Code _____ Class Number _____

Instructor _____

LESSON 11

In the blank space in the right-hand margin write the letter of the correct answer.

1. The first three chapters of Ephesians have as their theme
   a. the believer's battles in the heavenlies
   b. the believer's spiritual blessings in Christ
   c. the believer's assurance of material wealth and physical well-being in the Lord
   d. the believer's spiritual perils

2. Throughout eternity, the Church is to be
   a. the showpiece of God's wisdom
   b. the battleground between good and evil, right and wrong
   c. the one hope the lost have that they, too, will eventually be redeemed
   d. highly exalted, indeed made but "a little lower than the angels"

3. Paul was in prison when he wrote his epistle to the Philippians
   a. which explains why it has the "smell of a prison" about it
   b. yet it rings with rejoicing, praise and thanksgiving
   c. so Paul is to be excused for sounding an occasional note of discouragement
   d. and he was expecting to be executed shortly

12/7

4. What was Paul's attitude towards the religious accomplish-
ments, honors and attainments of his unconverted days? He
   a. gloried in them as real triumphs of his spirit over his flesh
   b. built on them as a firm and useful foundation for his
      Christian life
   c. counted them as loss and liability for Christ
   d. ignored them and never talked about them

5. The letter to the Colossians was written to
   a. help keep the Colossian Christians in the traditional paths
      of Christianity
   b. tell the Colossians not to neglect keeping the ordinances
   c. warn the Colossians against any abandonment of the Law
      of Moses
   d. exalt Christ as the answer to any leanings towards error

6. The prevailing theme of I Thessalonians is
   a. the danger of heresy
   b. the way of salvation
   c. the second coming of Christ
   d. the need for evangelism

7. In 2 Thessalonians Paul
   a. says that the "Day of the Lord" has already come
   b. writes about the coming of the man of sin, the Anti-
      christ
   c. denies the doctrine of the rapture of the Church
   d. does all the above

8. In I Timothy, Paul
   a. warns Timothy not to abandon the faith
   b. refrains from any reference to Timothy's personal ministry
   c. lays great stress on Church order
   d. urges Timothy to come to Rome and minister to him in
      prison

9. In the epistle written by Paul during his last imprisonment, Paul
    a. urges his readers to refrain from doing anything to incur the wrath of the government since such action might prejudice his chances of escaping execution
    b. tells the Christians to practice civil disobedience as a legitimate way of obtaining their constitutional rights
    c. rejoices that, despite all its difficulties, the Church was at least free from apostasy
    d. foresees increasing wickedness to be a chief characteristic of the last days

10. Who was the runaway slave, saved in Rome through the ministry of the apostle Paul and sent back by Paul to his master, who happened to be one of Paul's personal friends?
    a. Philemon
    b. Onesimus
    c. Epaphroditus
    d. Titus
    e. Archippus

WHAT DO YOU SAY?

Read Philemon. What was the greatest blow against slavery struck by Paul in this brief note? In the light of this epistle, what should be the Christian's attitude to social injustices?

Onesimus was a slave before he was saved
After he was Saved he became the "Brother" in christ
we need to consider all believers as brothers
and Sisters and forgave and love one another
as christ did to us.

LESSON 12

In the blank space in the right-hand margin write the letter of the correct answer.

11. To understand the epistle to the Hebrews we must remember that
     a. it is possible for a truly saved person to be lost again
     b. it was written to explain to Hebrew Christians the nature of Gentile Christianity
     c. when it was written the Temple was still standing in Jerusalem and Jewish Christians were under constant pressure and temptation to return to Judaism
     d. Christianity is a logical extension of Judaism and therefore as much of the Jewish religion as possible needed to be retained in the new faith

C

12. Which of the following titles would best suit the Epistle of James?
     a. God Is Still on the Throne
     b. Hold Your Tongue
     c. A Belief That Behaves
     d. Work for the Night Is Coming

C

13. The background to Peter's first epistle was
     a. the suffering and persecution through which many of the believers were passing at the time
     b. the materialism and worldiness of the Church
     c. the drabness, coldness and sterilized orthodoxy of so many Christians
     d. the battle between "conservatives" in the Church, led by Peter, who wanted to retain as much as possible of Judaism and "liberals," led by Paul, who demanded complete freedom from Judaism

A

14. Peter's second epistle emphasizes one characteristic of latter-day infidels. According to Peter these apostates will deny
     a. the virgin birth of the Lord Jesus
     b. the vicarious, atoning death of the Lord Jesus
     c. the bodily resurrection of the Lord Jesus
     d. the second coming of the Lord Jesus

D

12/10

15. John's first epistle emphasizes throughout
   a. the blessed hope of the Lord's return
   b. the emancipation of the Christian from the Law of Moses
   c. the features of family life in Christ
   d. the impossibility of any lasting assurance of salvation so long as we are in the body

   _C_

16. Where in John's writings are we told to close the door to false teachers? In
   a. John's Gospel
   b. I John
   c. II John
   d. III John
   e. Revelation

   _C_

17. Jude uses three characters from the Old Testament to illustrate three types of apostasy. Core illustrates the wickedness of
   a. making money out of divine matters
   b. any form of human religion
   c. leavening Biblical truth with false doctrine
   d. rebellion against God's order and rule
   e. tolerating immorality in the Church
   f. setting up graven images as objects of worship or veneration

   _D_

18. The letters to the seven Churches
   a. deal with matters pertaining to seven literal churches existing in John's day
   b. anticipate the entire course of the Church age
   c. embrace both the above
   d. have to do with neither of the above but deal with groups of believers gathering for worship and fellowship during the period of the Great Tribulation

   _C_

19. The period in Revelation covered by the seals, trumpets and vials
   a. relates to the time immediately prior to the Lord's coming for the Church
   b. is a period of great joy on earth as the Lord pours out from heaven one blessing after another
   c. embraces a terrible time yet to come in this world's history and generally known as "the time of Jacob's trouble"
   d. shows that the Gospel will eventually triumph on earth as it gradually converts the whole of mankind and ushers in the Golden Age

   _C_

20. At the end of His earthly reign, the Lord Jesus
    a. will return to heaven after having first anointed David to be His vice-regent on earth
    b. judge the wicked of all ages and consign them to a lost eternity
    c. allow godless men to take over the earth and work out their unhappy destiny without hindrance or restraint
    d. smite the earth with a curse as foretold in the last book of the Old Testament _____ B

WHAT DO YOU SAY?

How has this course helped you?

Very much. It is really very interesting to study the Scripture in short but very profitable. I learned many new things. I thank God and praise the Lord for Jesus Christ as my Lord and Saviour — Amen —

SUGGESTIONS FOR CLASS USE
OF SELF-CHECK TESTS

1. The class teacher may wish to tear out this page from each student textbook as the answer key is on the reverse side.

2. The class teacher should do the Self-Check Tests ahead of the class, correcting his own answers. He will then be able to help the class during the lesson on some of the harder questions.

3. Self-Check Tests can be used as a review of the lesson. A few minutes can be taken at the beginning of the class session to take the Test for the previous week's lesson. The tests can then be quickly graded by having the teacher call out the correct answers. A brief discussion of the answers serves as excellent review.

4. Everything should be done to encourage each class member to take the Tests and Exams. This is the way to learn.

5. Some recognition should be given to those who successfully complete this course.

ANSWER KEY TO SELF-CHECK TESTS

Be sure to look up any questions you have answered incorrectly. The page number is given after each question in the test. Mark with an "x" your wrong answers.

SELF-CHECK TEST

Test	1	2	3	4	5	6	7	8	9	10	11	12
Question 1	T	F	F	F	T	F	T	T	T	T	T	F
2	T	T	T	F	F	F	T	F	T	F	F	T
3	F	F	F	T	F	T	T	T	T	T	T	F
4	F	T	T	T	T	T	F	T	T	T	T	T
5	T	T	T	T	T	F	F	F	F	F	F	F
6	T	T	T	T	T	T	T	T	F	T	T	T
7	F	T	F	T	T	T	T	T	F	F	T	F
8	T	F	T	T	F	F	T	T	T	F	F	T
9	F	F	F	F	T	T	T	F	T	F	T	F
10	T	T	T	F	F	F	T	F	T	T	T	F
Number of questions correct	10	10	8	9	10	9	10	9	8	9	7	10
Multiply by ten	x10	x10	x10	x10	x10	x10	x10	x10	x10	x10	x10	x10
Your score	100	100	80	90	100	90	100	90	80	90	70	100

100%   Excellent work.
90%   Very good work. Check the ones you answered incorrectly.
80%   Good work. Reread the lesson.
Less than 80%. Study the lesson again.